OFFSHORE
SALT WATER FISHING

LEARN FROM
THE EXPERTS AT

MAGAZINE

CREATIVE
PUBLISHING
international

MINNETONKA, MINNESOTA

www.creativepub.com

5900 Green Oak Drive
Minnetonka, MN 55343
1-800-328-3895
www.creativepub.com

Offshore Salt Water Fishing
Introduction by Barry Gibson, Editor, SALT WATER SPORTSMAN

Executive Editor, Outdoor Group: David R. Maas
Senior Editor and Project Leader: Steven Hauge
Managing Editor: Jill Anderson
Creative Director: Brad Springer
Project Manager and Photo Editor: Angela Hartwell
Copy Editors: Barry Gibson, Janice Cauley
Staff Photographer: Tate Carlson
Director, Production Services: Kim Gerber
Production Manager: Helga Thielen
Production Staff: Stephanie Barakos, Laura Hokkanen

Special thanks to: Barry Gibson, Tom Richardson, Chris Powers and the staff of
Salt Water Sportsman magazine

Cover Credits: *Tuna Surprise* painting by Don Ray; background schooling tuna
photo by Mark Conlin/Seapics.com; front cover photos: Evelyn Letfuss: left,
Tom Richardson: right; back cover photos: William Boyce: left, Bill Lindner
Photography: center, Scott Kerrigan: right

Contributing Photographers: Dan Blanton, William Boyce, Eleonora de
Sabata/Seapics.com, Richard Gibson, Richard Herrmann, Scott Kerrigan, Gary
Kramer, Larry Larsen, Evelyn Letfuss, Bill Lindner Photography, Dick Mermon,
Randy Morse/Herrmann Pix, Tony Peña, George Poveromo, Tom Richardson,
Al Ristori, Philip Rosenberg, Lenny Rudow, David J. Sams/Texas Inprint, Bob
Stearns, Sam Talarico, Art Womack

Contributing Illustrators: Chris Armstrong, Dan Daly, John F. Eggert, Joe Fahey,
Dave McHose, Diane Rome Peebles, John Rice, David Shepherd, Tom Waters

Printed on American Paper by: R. R. Donnelley & Sons Co.

10 9 8 7 6 5 4 3 2 1

Library of Congress Cataloging-in-Publication Data

Offshore salt water fishing : learn from the experts at Salt water sportsman magazine.
    p. cm.
  ISBN 1-58923-010-8 (hardcover)
   1. Saltwater fishing. I. Creative Publishing International. II. Salt water sportsman.
SH457 .O33 2002
799.1'6--dc21
                         2001054816

Table of Contents

Introduction

Broadbill Swordfish

It's well past noon, and the sun has become a brilliant laser beam piercing down from a cobalt sky. It's oppressively hot and humid, and the boat's gentle motion as it glides over the somnolent swells, along with the low throbbing of the engines, is hypnotizing. But nothing's happening. Despite the fresh, expertly rigged baits deployed just after daybreak and which have been faithfully inspected or changed every 30 minutes, not a single fish has been seen in nearly seven hours of trolling. Your eyelids become increasingly heavy as you struggle to stay focused on your offerings skipping along at the edge of the prop wash, but you're losing the battle. Hey, a short snooze wouldn't hurt, would it...?

"There it is! Left rigger!" comes the cry from the flybridge, jarring you to your senses and propelling you to your feet. A dark, three-foot-long bill emerges from a boil of white water and slashes wildly at the skirted ballyhoo. Then the fish disappears, only to materialize seconds later behind the chin-weighted mackerel on the right flat line. Fully lit-up in neon purple stripes, dorsal fin erect and pectorals extended, the behemoth lunges forward, engulfs the bait, and vanishes into the depths. Fifty-pound mono, crackling under the strain of the drag, streams off the two-speed reel as you struggle to free the bucking rod from its holder and secure the butt into your fighting belt. Just as you clip the second harness strap to the reel lug, 300 pounds of berserk blue marlin clears the water off the starboard beam and greyhounds away in bursts of spray. Crewmembers frantically crank in the other lines as the skipper spins the boat to keep the fish off the stern. At this point it's all you can do just to hang on, and you know it's going to be a while – maybe hours – before this fish will be brought to boatside. And that's if everything goes right.

Make no mistake about it, offshore fishing is the most exciting facet of salt water angling.

The savage strike of a billfish, wahoo, kingfish, or outsized dolphin provides a rush of adrenaline that few other species can impart, and the slug-it-out battle tactics of a big shark, tuna or swordfish will test your stamina and tackle to the max. And to top it off, these gamesters don't grow to proportions that put them at the top of the food chain – some can weigh upwards of a half-ton – by being careless. Many have superb eyesight and other advanced senses that help them detect the slightest irregularity in a potential meal. And therein lies the challenge for the offshore angler – to create and present a bait or lure that will fool some of nature's wariest denizens into striking.

But today we have advantages as never before. Reliable, high-tech sportfishing boats – even affordable and trailerable 25-foot center consoles – get us to the offshore grounds quickly, and allow us to fish in comfort when we arrive. Modern electronics make navigation and fishfinding a snap, and provide a level of safety inconceivable just a decade ago. Rods, reels and accessories are at the cutting edge of technology, as is the tackle. Ultra-thin titanium leaders, nearly invisible fluorocarbon lines, and chemically sharpened hooks give us an unprecedented edge, and the vast array of artificial lures offered in stores and catalogs is truly mind-boggling. It has never been easier to get geared up for blue-water sport.

Yet, despite all these accouterments, it still takes more than a modicum of knowledge and skill to ensure success on the offshore grounds. Natural baits must be rigged flawlessly and presented perfectly, artificials have to be worked "just so" for maximum productivity, and special tricks and tactics are often needed when fish get finicky. And that's why *Offshore Salt Water Fishing* is such an invaluable reference. Authored by some of the most celebrated experts in the business including George Poveromo, Al Ristori, Capt. Mike "Beak" Hurt, Angelo Cuanang, and John Brownlee.

Each of the 31 chapters has appeared as an acclaimed feature article in *Salt Water Sportsman* magazine and is packed with solid how-to information. These hands-on pros will show you how to zero-in on the top dozen oceanic gamesters, and explain in detail specialized techniques such as wire lining, kite fishing, deep-jigging, gaffing, dealing with rough sea conditions and catching live bait. Along the way you'll meet plenty of seasoned charter skippers and tournament contenders, each eager to share what he's learned over the years in order to help you become a more proficient offshore angler.

One thematic thread that runs through the book is that of conservation. Open-ocean (or "highly migratory") fish have come under increasing pressure from industrial-scale commercial fishing operations, and stocks of several species are seriously depleted and in need of rebuilding. A number of pro-active groups such as The Billfish Foundation, the National Coalition for Marine Conservation, and the Recreational Fishing Alliance work diligently to pass new laws to curtail overfishing, and are pushing for sensible plans that will protect these great gamesters in the years to come. We, as anglers, can do our part as well. We need to carefully release all billfish and undersized fish of any species. We should consider using circle hooks. We can participate in a tagging program that will provide vital information to researchers and fishery managers. We can join and support the above-mentioned organizations. And finally, we can simply limit our catch on each trip to what we can reasonably use. That's key.

Offshore, blue-water fishing. It's the pinnacle of salt water sport, the ultimate in angling excitement, and always an adventure!

Barry Gibson, Editor
SALT WATER SPORTSMAN

Billfish

BLUE MARLIN

Blue Marlin

The largest and most widely distributed member of the billfish family, blue marlin are thought to reach weights in excess of 2000 pounds and exceed 15 feet in length. Known for their spectacular fighting ability, blues can be airborne one minute and on deep, sounding runs the next.

The top areas to catch blue marlin are Hawaii, Mexico, Australia and East Africa, with Madeira and the Azores being hot spots for big fish.

Striped Marlin

The colorful striped marlin is recognized for the beautiful blue-to-purple vertical stripes on its sides, which are typically more prominent than on other marlin species. Growing to 500 pounds, the striped marlin is a great fighter and often spends as much time in the air as in the water when hooked.

The best areas to find striped marlin include Baja, Mexico, Costa Rica, Hawaii and New Zealand.

Black Marlin

Because of a more limited distribution, black marlin are not as popular as blue, white or striped marlin. But where they are found, the black marlin is known as a tough fighter that can reach sizes nearing that of the blue marlin. As their name would suggest, black marlin have a deep blue or black back, a light-colored belly with a short heavy bill.

The best fishing for black marlin occurs in the waters off Australia, Costa Rica, Panama and Peru.

Sailfish

Easily recognized by their large dorsal "sail" and long pelvic fins, the aptly named sailfish are classified as the Atlantic or Pacific variety. The primary difference in the two is their maximum size, with the Pacific sailfish reaching 220 pounds and the Atlantic 140 pounds.

The best areas to catch sailfish are Brazil, Florida, Mexico and Venezuela in the Atlantic and Costa Rica, Ecuador, Mexico and Panama in the Pacific.

White Marlin

The smallest of the marlin species; a large white marlin will weigh under 200 pounds. However, they more than make up for their small size with an aggressive nature and great jumping ability.

Found in the Atlantic Ocean, top locations include the Bahamas, Bermuda, the Eastern coast of the United States, Florida and Costa Rica.

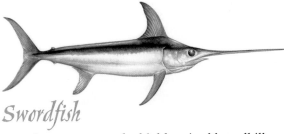

Swordfish

In recent years the highly-prized broadbill swordfish has primarily been the target of offshore commercial fishermen. Populations in many areas have been decimated, and the number of large specimens available is very limited.

There are only a few areas where broadbills are intentionally fished for with rod and reel, often at night. These areas include Chile, Mexico, the Northeast coast of the United States, South Florida and occasionally Southern California.

BILLFISH:
Red, White and Atlantic Blue

by Tom Richardson

*Five experts from around the country share their secrets
for finding Atlantic blue marlin in U.S. waters.*

f you fish offshore anywhere from Massachusetts to Texas, the odds of catching a blue marlin in your home waters may be better than you think. However, the trick to finding them is knowing the right kinds of "marlin signs" to look for, so you can narrow your search.

In the following article we interview five captains from different parts of the coast to see how they go about hunting blue marlin. Their methods and advice, while somewhat different for each captain, can also be applied to whichever part of the coast that you fish. Also, this information is useful for finding other species of offshore game fish that are found in the same areas as marlin.

The experts' home bases

Point Pleasant, New Jersey

Oregon Inlet, North Carolina

Destin, Florida

Galveston, Texas

Key West, Florida

Galveston, Texas

Blue marlin can be caught off Texas throughout the year, but strong winds and rough seas keep most people from venturing offshore during the winter. The season usually begins in March, April and May, when lots of small marlin move through the area. This initial run eventually gives way to larger, but fewer, fish during the summer. Fall brings the year's best marlin fishing.

"My favorite time to fish is during the fall," says Capt. Howard Horton, who fishes out of Galveston. "That's when you see a lot of bigger fish moving through, and they seem to be in shallower water."

Horton, a respected competitor in the Texas tournament circuit, is quick to point out that you don't have to be in deep water to find marlin. In fact, the biggest marlin he's seen was in 55 fathoms, and he's found them as close in as 25 fathoms. "The oil platforms in 65 to 75 fathoms produce too," he says.

Horton has a list of favorite marlin hot spots, which include platforms, wrecks, reefs, seamounts and drop-offs. However, if Horton runs across what he calls "marlin water," he'll drop his baits right there. Marlin water is clear, blue water containing lots of baitfish. "The depth is not as important as clarity," Horton says, adding that water temperature alone is not an important factor. In fact, Horton has caught marlin in water ranging from 77 degrees into the 90s. What's most important is finding the temperature breaks. "If I'm in warm water, I'll look for cool water; and if I'm in cool water, I'll look for warm water," he says.

Horton says he's learned a lot by listening to ocean long-liners, commercial fishermen who work far out at sea. They've told him to pay attention to any kind of change in the water surface, be it temperature breaks, slicks, rips or grass lines. "Any sort of change is good."

He also likes to troll along grass lines, which baitfish use for protection. Catching a dolphin or wahoo along the grass is a good sign that marlin are also in the area. "We have a saying in Texas: Find a 'hoo and you'll find a blue," he told me with a chuckle, then added hastily, "Hey, I didn't come up with it."

Oil rigs are another form of East Coast and Gulf of Mexico structure that holds baitfish, small tunas and the marlin that eat them. "The platforms are a McDonald's for fish," says Horton. "Stick around long enough and something will happen." Also, don't overlook the mooring buoys near the platforms, since they also hold tuna and marlin.

Speaking of tunas, vast schools of blackfins are often encountered off Texas, and it's usually a good bet there's a marlin lurking around them. The tunas Horton most likes to see are the five- to ten-pound blackfins, known in Texas as "marlin muffins." Blackfins will often feed on the surface in schools spanning 200 square yards. To fish them, Horton trolls around the edges of the school.

Bottom structure is also important to Horton, since the irregular contour creates upwellings that hold baitfish. He mentions hot spots such as the Peanut, the Flower Gardens, the Colt 45 seamount, the BP-rig seamount and the 100-fathom curve.

A good depthsounder is very important when working bottom structure, since you've got to find the bait if you want to find the marlin. If he marks a good concentration of baitfish directly on top of the structure, Horton trolls in a crisscross fashion over the area. If the bait is bunched up on the edge, he'll circle it.

Work the area long enough, and the bait will often come to the surface. This often happens early in the morning and in the evening. "My favorite time of day to fish is the last two hours of the day," says Horton. "That's when the water starts cooling off and the bait comes to the surface. Then it's easier to see and work the schools."

Birds are important indicators of fish activity, and Horton keeps an eye out for two species in particular: boobies and petrels. "Two or three boobies diving is a good sign," he says. "The bait may be deep, but it's there. Those birds have excellent vision." The tiny petrels are even better. "Five or six of them working the surface is real good. It's a sure sign that fish are under them. If you see them sitting on the water, it often means that there have been fish feeding in the area. Stick around and they'll come back up, or work the area and try to locate the bait on your fishfinder."

The best conditions for marlin fishing, according to Horton, are overcast skies with a 3- to 5-foot chop. He feels both factors help disguise the bait and hide the leader and hooks. Wind direction affects the fishing too. For instance, off Galveston, Horton likes a southwest or west-southwest wind not exceeding 12 knots, which blows in warmer, cleaner water from the open Gulf. East winds can be a problem if there is heavy runoff from the Mississippi. Finally, Horton believes that a low or falling barometer makes for more marlin action offshore.

As for moon phase, Horton likes to fish the two days before and after the full moon, and one day on either side of the new moon, since these phases mean the most water movement in terms of tidal current.

Most of all, Horton believes that confidence has a lot to do with success. "If you have a particular lure or bait that you know has caught fish before, stick with it," he says emphatically. "Don't go changing baits every 30 minutes.

"It's hard to explain, but if you have confidence in a particular bait, you'll work a little harder. If you have a system that works, stick with it – it will catch fish."

The same is true when fishing a favorite hot spot. If it has produced before and the conditions are roughly the same, keep working the area. If you don't hear of anything better going on elsewhere, stick around. Something will happen.

Destin, Florida

Destin is a small town on the northwest coast of Florida, but it's one of the largest fishing centers in the country, with over 150 boats available for charter. It's where you'll find Capt. John Holley of the charter boat *Invicta*. Holley has won the award for the top sport fishing captain in the Destin Fishing Rodeo five years in a row, and is an expert blue-water fisherman.

Blue marlin have been caught every month of the year off Destin, but most people start looking for them beginning in early May, when water temperatures become most favorable. Holley likes them to be in the mid-70s, and feels anything lower than 70 degrees runs the fish off. Good marlin fishing is had right through the summer, and generally ends around the first week in November.

According to Holley, the local marlin fishery can really be divided into two distinct "seasons." "From May through mid-July, I like to target the blue water and the grass lines," he says. "During this time, especially in June, is when you find blue water closest to shore, sometimes as close in as 30 fathoms."

Like Horton, Holley is quick to dispel the myth that you can only find marlin in deep water. "If I can't find any weedlines or bait, I'll cruise the rock formations and ledges in 30 to 40 fathoms." The bait that congregates around this rocky underwater structure will attract marlin, and it's often where the first fish of the season is caught. There's actually more fish close to land if there are no weeds and bait to hold them on the surface offshore.

Holley says ocean-temperature charts are helpful for locating the edges of blue water; if you find a break in the water temperature, you'll usually find a weedline.

After mid-July, the blue water usually shifts farther offshore, and the remarkable second phase of the marlin fishery begins. In midsummer, enormous whale sharks move into the green water to feed on plankton in the Elbow and Dump areas in 100 fathoms. The area is also packed with small baitfish, which attract bonito (little tunny) and small blackfin tuna. Just outside the perimeter of these fish are skipjacks and small yellowfins, followed by larger yellowfins and marlin. Each feeding whale shark marks the center of a huge swirling food chain.

"I'll start off by moving from shark to shark, and work each school with a trolling lure, trying to catch the "easy" fish and cover more ground. Then I'll pick a few good schools and troll a live bait (one of the 10- to 15-pound tuna) around them." The whale shark pattern is generally at its peak through August and into September. Then, after the first two cold fronts blow through, they disappear.

Fishing over bottom structure drop-offs, seamounts and ledges is another good way to score a marlin. A perennial hot spot is the Spur, just inshore of De-Soto Canyon. This is a small "hook" on the bottom contour, from 300 to 400 fathoms, where most of the big blue marlin off Destin have been caught. The Florida state record blue of 980 pounds was caught in June, 1985, in the DeSoto. June and July are the prime months for fishing DeSoto Canyon and the Spur. Another productive piece of structure is the underwater mountain offshore of the Spur that rises 50 fathoms off the bottom.

Birds also play an important role in Holley's fishing strategy. "I'll always steer toward a single man-o'-war [frigate] bird that's circling, because it could be following a big fish," adding that he also looks for the small petrels, known as tuna birds, which fly low to the water and are a good sign that tuna schools are in the area.

Over the years, Holley has found that the best times for marlin fishing are the hour and a half following sunrise and then again at high noon. Best winds for Destin fishing are from the southeast or east; those out of the west are terrible.

Like Horton, Holley prefers a falling barometer to rising, but his opinion on moon phase differs slightly. "Typically, I like to fish on the full and new moons," he says. "I guess I'd have to say the downside of the full moon – the three days after – is the worst. The best time would be from the new moon building toward the full."

Holley prefers scattered clouds and sunshine for marlin fishing, but does not like total overcast. Intermittent showers passing through the area are very good too, he says. "It seems that the edges of isolated showers will turn the fish on. I'll actually locate pockets of these clouds on my radar and fish them." He says the showers are "something a little bit different," which always seem to be a good place to find fish. In other words, look for something different from the norm, be it a small rise on the bottom, a whale shark or a change in water color.

Holley makes an interesting comparison to freshwater bass fishing, which he used to do a lot of. "In bass fishing, we always tried to pick a point along a stump field or weedbed. The same thing is true in marlin fishing. For instance, if we find a "V" in a weedline where two currents come together, the fish will often be around that "V", either on the point or in the pocket."

Key West, Florida

Norm Wood is best known as the captain who, in the 1970s, pioneered blue marlin fishing along the section of the Pourtales Escarpment now known as Wood's Wall, which lies 18 miles south of Key West.

According to Wood, October and November are the hottest months for marlin fishing along the Wall, when he believes that the fish are migrating south after summering in the East Coast canyons. He says a northeast wind is best at this time, because it pushes cooler water and baitfish into the area. In fact, any wind from the eastern quadrants is considered good in Wood's opinion, while anything from the west is bad.

There's also a small run of fish in late April/early May, which Wood believes are moving north. The biggest fish are caught in the winter months, but they are not common.

In the fall, small tunas show up along the Wall, along with tightly packed pods of small baitfish that can be marked on the fishfinder. Wood looks for water temperatures from 78 to 80 degrees for marlin. When it gets into the high 80s, as it often does in summer, the water gets stagnant and so does the fishing.

Bait is a key consideration when marlin fishing,

according to Wood. Small dolphins along the weed-lines are good signs, as are rips and porpoises. Wood says frigate birds can lead you to billfish from April to August, but that boobies are not too dependable. He likes a little chop on the water, with moderate seas best. Overcast or sunny, the sky condition doesn't seem to matter.

Wood stresses the importance of moon phase in the Wall fishery. Unlike most spots in the Atlantic, the downside of the moon – the quarter moon – seems to spark the best fishing. "Action drops off noticeably during the full moon periods," says Wood, who puts a lot of stock in the lunar prime times. Prime time occurs an hour before to an hour after when the moon is directly overhead or directly on the opposite side of the earth. Also, Wood says the half hour before and after the time when the moon is just coming up or going down are productive times to fish. These are the times to be at your favorite hot spots. (Lunar prime times are published in some papers and magazines.)

Top spots to fish along the Wall are the three cracks, or fissures, in the Wall where the bait tends to stack up. The East Crack is best because the Wall drops off the steepest – from 850 feet to 1,500 feet.

Most of all, Wood says to listen to other anglers. "Best thing is to keep track of what people are doing out there," he says. "Keep your ears open."

Oregon Inlet, North Carolina

Capt. Chip Schaefer of Oregon Inlet, North Carolina, certainly agrees with him. Here, too, they catch marlin year-round, but the peak season off Oregon Inlet really starts around the last week in May or early June and runs well into September.

From June to July, boats concentrate along the 100-fathom curve and fish in the Gulf Stream itself, usually along a 35-mile stretch from The Point to the Diamond Shoals Light Tower. The Point is a sharp contour in the shelf where the Gulf Stream veers off the 100-fathom curve toward the northeast, and a lot of action seems to occur around it. During this initial period, boats will troll up and down the Stream, anywhere from 100 fathoms out to 500 fathoms.

From July until the end of the season, the time when most big blues are caught, Schaefer and the other captains out of Oregon Inlet concentrate on the area northeast of Oregon Inlet, where white

willingness of local captains to share their knowledge of where the fish are and what they've been hitting.

He says that bright, blue water is always good, but don't rule out green or off-color water. The 100-fathom line is usually a good bet, but he points out that marlin have also been caught in 50 fathoms all the way out to 1,400 fathoms. Finding a concentration of baitfish (bonito, sardines, squid) is ideal, he says, but he won't necessarily leave the area if he doesn't see schools on the surface or mark any on his fishfinder. Again, it all depends on where the fish have been caught recently, and getting info from other captains is the easiest and surest way of locating the most productive areas.

When pressed, there are some factors that Schaefer admits will produce better marlin fishing. For instance, he says that a strong current in the Gulf Stream, say four or five knots, is terrible for marlin fishing, while a light current is very good. As far as the moon phase is concerned, he says that marlin have been caught during all phases; however, "a day or two before the fullmoon in August may give you a little bit of an edge." And that "the full moon in August is a pregnant time for big blue marlin."

When asked about weather conditions, Schaefer says "it can never get too pretty." A sunny, flat-calm day is wonderful for white and blue marlin fishing northeast of Oregon Inlet. Also, it allows him to see the fish under the baits more easily. Northeast or easterly winds seem to produce good fishing, particularly the die-out of a northeaster. The prevailing southwest wind in the spring is good, too, especially in the Gulf Stream fishery. Generally, a west or southwest wind is least favored and "a rainy southeast wind is a sorry day to fish, but the die-out can be good."

The presence of birds is always a good sign that something is happening, says Schaefer, who puts the most faith in shearwaters and Corey's petrels, not the smaller Wilson's petrels. "When you see the

marlin are also abundant. Here the fishing isn't done in the main current of the Gulf Stream, which flows far offshore, but over and along the edge of the continental shelf where the water is sometimes "blended." July serves as a transition month, when blues can be caught both to the northeast of Oregon Inlet and in the Stream.

Schaefer doesn't put a lot of stock in most popular marlin theories when it comes to the North Carolina fishery. He says that marlin have been caught in all kinds of conditions and situations when by most traditional standards they shouldn't have. For instance, while many captains in the region feel that 78 degrees is the magic temperature for marlin, Schaefer points out that fish have been caught in water ranging from 68 to 83 degrees. As for the ocean-temperature charts, Schaefer says they may be useful, but that he doesn't use them himself.

So what water temp is best? "The type that the fish have been caught in recently," says Schaefer. It may sound simplistic, but it's indicative of Schaefer's marlin-fishing philosophy.

The main criteria in choosing a spot is where the action has been lately – "what's been going on," says Schaefer. "Listen to what everybody else is doing." This means talking to other captains at the dock and listening to radio chatter. "We're pretty open-ended on the radio off North Carolina," he says of the

Corey's circling tight, it's a good sign that there's life in the area," he says.

From August into the fall, the marlin captains look for Gulf Stream fingers to bring blue water into the northeast area. These fingers can be very important to the fishing. Sometimes a northeast wind will isolate pockets of this warm, bait-rich blue water and produce excellent fishing. When a finger pushes inshore, Schaefer advises working the edges and the middle of the blue-water zone.

In closing, Schaefer makes one final note. He says that if you wanted to pick the time of day when marlin action is generally best, it would be from 11:00 a.m. to 2:30 p.m. – right in the middle of the day.

Point Pleasant, New Jersey

Blue marlin are not common in the Northeast, but even fishermen out of Massachusetts ports occasionally find them in the canyons. Paul Regula, a charter captain from Point Pleasant, New Jersey, spends an estimated 150 days on the water, 35 to 40 of them in the canyons. While he stresses the rarity of catching a blue marlin, he says that the ones in the Northeast tend to be bigger fish weighing over 500 pounds. A lot of marlin are lost or missed because the majority of fishermen are using tackle and tactics aimed at tuna.

You'll find marlin in the same areas that you'll find tuna, so Regula always looks for temperature breaks and clean, blue water. "If you find a rip with 69.5 degrees on one side and 72 on the other, that's magic," says Regula enthusiastically. While tuna can usually be found on the cool-water side of a temperature break, Regula has found that marlin tend to stay on the warmer side; however, that doesn't mean they won't cross the barrier to chase a meal.

Baitfish presence is also important, as is structure. The ideal situation is to find a temperature break on the edge of the canyon shelf with lots of bait. The presence of bait is of utmost importance, because the game fish won't stay where there isn't any food.

Regula says to pay particular attention to anything unusual in the ocean, no matter how small. "The ocean is pretty much a boring place," he says. "Pay attention to dumb things, like a piece of rope floating in the water or a chum bucket."

Such flotsam, while seemingly insignificant, will

attract and hold life. For example, the floating chum bucket may contain a few trigger fish. Below the bucket may be dolphin or tuna, and below these fish may be a marlin. If you come across an object floating in the water and there are no other signs to work with, fish the area thoroughly.

Offshore rips are particularly good places to fish because they indicate current edges and upwellings. These often produce plankton blooms, which hold bait and game fish. Last year, Regula said he could actually see the rips on his radar screen on flat-calm days.

An abundance of dolphin and weeds in an area is a good sign that marlin may be present. Also, be on the alert if you see a lot of skipjacks; "they're candy for blue marlin," says Regula.

Frigate birds also show up during the season, and have been known to track a single marlin, waiting for it to feed. Also, Regula says to pay attention to shearwaters and Mother Cary's chickens (stormy petrels), especially if there's a slick under them.

The canyon season really starts when a warm-water eddy from the Gulf Stream swings in along the edge of the continental shelf. That's why Regula uses ocean-temperature charts religiously. "Satellite coverage is indispensable."

Canyon action usually starts around the last week in July. If nothing looks promising on the temperature charts and he hasn't heard anything from other skippers, Regula may simply run to Lindenkohl Canyon and troll all the way to Hudson Canyon. He'll work a zigzag pattern from 500 to 1,000 fathoms and back again as he heads north. "It's sort of like a reconnaissance mission, I'm looking for something that doesn't show up on the charts."

When asked about the best sea conditions for marlin, Regula said he likes the water choppy as opposed to flat calm. He thinks the water motion may oxygenate the surface water, and the fish may actually get "juiced" on it.

Wind direction can also affect the fishing. Best winds for the canyons are from the east, since they push the warm Gulf Stream water toward shore, creating upwellings. A wind blowing from the southwest or west usually means poor fishing because the cooler, darker inshore water is pushed over the warm water.

Canyon Target: Big Blue Marlin!

by Al Ristori

*More and more trophy-size blue marlin are being taken
— on purpose — out over the canyons of the Northeast.*

The blue marlin action that can be experienced in the canyons from New Jersey to southern New England is a wake-up call to those who assumed they'd have to travel to the Outer Banks of North Carolina or out of the country in order to catch a blue. You couldn't say that blue marlin are common, but they are far from being an unusual catch in northern canyons. Many Northeast captains and anglers have scored their first blue marlin in the last few years, and it's a sure bet that lots more will be making a special effort for one through the summer.

It's not too surprising when blue marlin are caught in the Wilmington, Baltimore and Washington canyons, which are fished regularly by boats out of Cape May, New Jersey. However, the more northerly canyons can produce. This fact is best illustrated by the experiences of Capt. Jody Di Stasio, who runs the *XTC* out of Belmar, New Jersey. Di Stasio has made 35 to 40 canyon trips (almost all overnighters) a season for many years, yet despite all that time on the water he had never even raised a blue marlin. That ended in the mid–nineties, when the same trolling techniques he had been using all along for bigeye tuna resulted in six blues hooked and two caught!

Di Stasio broke the ice during a July 31, 1994,

overnighter that saw Ralph Johnson of Shrewsbury, New Jersey, bring in a 254-pounder for mounting, while another blue was lost at Lindenkoehl Canyon. After that first-ever blue was boated, Di Stasio vowed never to kill another unless it was a possible tournament winner.

His resolve was put to the test during an overnighter in Toms Canyon on August 10. After a blue in the 300-pound class was lost that afternoon, Dave Bender of Manasquan, New Jersey, hooked a mystery fish at 7:00 p.m. Di Stasio assumed it was a large bigeye, because the fish never jumped. After an hour, however, a huge blue marlin surfaced.

Bender continued the fight into the dark, and it was another 45 minutes before the marlin was brought alongside. The *XTC*'s generator wouldn't start, so Di Stasio had to maneuver with very little light to work with, and there were only three people aboard to handle the fish. Still, it all worked out. The blue extended beyond the 13½-foot beam of the *XTC*, and Di Stasio estimated it at about 15 feet and around 1,000 pounds. Bender, a veteran big game angler, had never caught a blue before, but agreed with Di Stasio that he should set the fish free rather than try to challenge the New Jersey state record.

Di Stasio's other blue marlin action during early August also occurred in Toms Canyon. Every one of his six hookups came on Turbo Teaser lures. Some outrigger lures were hit, but the short lines saw the most action.

The fact that the *XTC* had two blues hooked during the same day indicates that northern blues aren't as unusual as many anglers may suspect. The year before, a couple of boats recorded two blue releases per day while fishing the northern canyons.

Not So Rare?

The fact is, big blues may be encountered in any of the canyons. The New Jersey state record is a 1,046-pounder caught by Dr. Phil Infantolino on his *Heart-to-Heart* out of Brielle Yacht Club. That fish was caught on August 2, 1986, while Infantolino was trolling the 1,000-fathom line in Hudson Canyon (the captain was John Frank). Infantolino's fish beat out a 972-pounder caught a few years before in Hudson Canyon by Jack Zaccone of Parsippany, New Jersey, while fishing on the *Huntress*.

The New York record was set on July 20 by Bill Sweedler of Westport, Connecticut, just a couple of weeks before Infantolino's catch. Sweedler's captain, Harry Clemenz, was trolling the 100-fathom line of the Fish Tail portion of Block Canyon when the 1,176-pound blue struck. It was finally landed after four hours and 25 minutes. During the fight the first rod broke and had to be tied to another line!

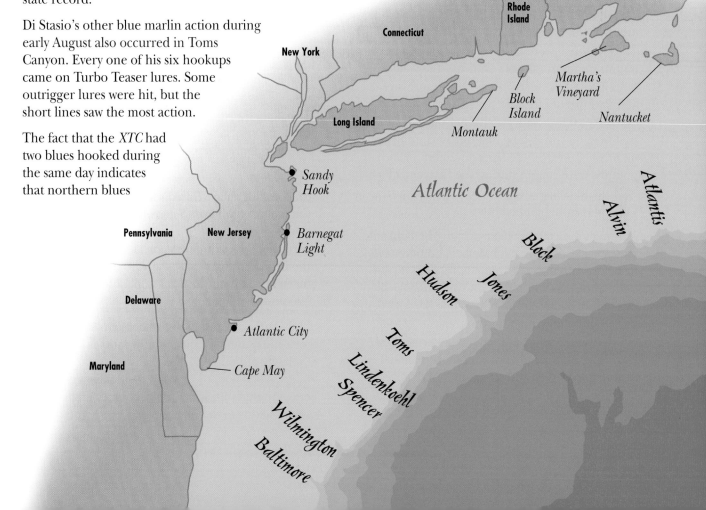

Big-Fish Stories

Several blues over 800 pounds have been boated in the northern canyons during the past 10 years, including a 1,028-pounder caught by Dom Pelusi on the *Kim Lauren II* out of Atlantic City. Since catches of large blues have become more common, and the conservation ethic has been pushed to the forefront, some exceptionally large blues have been released.

In addition to Bender's catch, Capt. Drew Santoro was trolling Dr. Seitzman's *Miss Shuga* from Brielle Yacht Club along the 100-fathom line of Hudson Canyon, when Tony Santoro (no relation to the captain) hooked a blue estimated to be in the 1,000-pound class. Santoro fought the fish for 1¾ hours before releasing it.

Blues have always been a more common catch for boats running out of South Jersey ports, and the $500,000 Mid-Atlantic Tournament out of The Canyon Club in Cape May emphasized that point. Though the first day of the mid-August contest was very rough and only 10 boats fished, the *Gold Rush* returned with a 497-pound blue. That set the tone for a contest that produced relatively few of the usually common white marlin, but an unexpected number of blues. The 142 boats, each fishing three days, scratched out only 197 whites, just a few of which were large enough to make the 60-pound minimum size. In contrast, the yield of 24 blues boated or released was most impressive – and that doesn't include the fish that were hooked and lost. Indeed, this may have been the best blue marlin fishing in a northern tournament since 17 fish, the largest weighing 836 pounds, were caught during the Leukemia Fish for Life Tournament out of Atlantic City and Cape May in the mid-eighties.

Although I've caught blue marlin in the Bahamas, Venezuela, Costa Rica and Mexico, I'd never even had a hookup with one in the states until the second day of 1994's Fish for Life Tournament, when a blue crashed a black-and-pink Schneider lure being trolled in Wilmington Canyon from the *Absolut-ly* out of Brielle Yacht Club. The blue started greyhounding for the horizon, and smoked off 400 yards from an 80W with 28 pounds of drag before the other lines were cleared and we were able to start backing down.

That incredible burst of energy took its toll on the fish, which we had seen wasn't that big. I retrieved line steadily for 15 minutes before the double appeared, and Big Mike Koblan and Michael Dinardi drew the blue alongside without a struggle. The reason soon became apparent: the fish had killed itself with that amazing run. It weighed 339 pounds and was well over the contest's 300-pound minimum, although it wasn't large enough to get on the board that day, one that saw seven blues brought in. However, our marlin did prove useful to a biologist who was taking samples from the dead billfish. In its stomach he found two large oceanic puffers, six small skipjacks and a large needlefish.

In that same tournament, Bernard and Drew Dinardi, veteran canyon anglers who took the top two tuna spots in the 1993 Mid-Atlantic Tournament, joined the ranks of those who recorded their first blue marlin last summer. Among the second-day catches were a 542-pounder on the *Princess Lily*, a 522-pounder on the *Kingfisher* and a 423-pounder that *Catalyst* skipper Russ Binns found for Ken Lindenman at the 500-fathom line of the Baltimore Canyon.

Tourneys Tell the Tale

There were few blues brought in after the second day of the Mid-Atlantic $500,000, because, as Tournament Director Dick Weber explained that night, there was such a big fish in first place. However, on the last afternoon, Fred Dombrow on the *Dulcinea* fought a 586-pound blue for 2¾ hours at the 1,000-fathom curve of Poorman's Canyon, and wound up taking the $196,525 first prize (including official calcuttas) for blue marlin.

The *Salt Water Sportsman* championship trophy in that contest went to Capt. Herb Schoenberg and the crew of the *Harry II* out of Beach Haven, who released a blue, as well as some white marlin, to earn the most points. The previous weekend, at the Ocean City overnighter, Schoenberg boated a 626-pound blue, and also caught another close to 500 pounds!

Rick Weber, at South Jersey Marina in Cape May, feels the number of blue marlin catches has gone up lately, although he isn't seeing the extra-large blues of 800 pounds or more that were being encountered during the 1980s. There seems to be some validity to that speculation, backed up by recent state records (discounting fish that were released) and tournament winners, both of which have shown that the marlin were a bit smaller. Still, the expectation of being able to catch a blue is now so high that South Jersey Marina has added a Blue Marlin Invitational Tournament to their schedule, from July 13 to 16.

Looking at catches over the last 10 years, that timing may be a tad early. Some blues have been caught from northern canyons in June, and a warm-water eddy spinning off from the Gulf Stream could bring tropical species in as early as May. July is probably the first fairly dependable month, but August seems to be the best bet.

Late-Summer Action

Labor Day weekend can be very good for blues, too. September catches dropped off sharply, but that's probably due to a lack of effort rather than a lack of fish. Pete Fisher set up a $5,000-entry blue marlin tournament at Montauk Marine Basin for September, since that was the month he figured would be best for big blues. Only three boats entered, but Fisher proved his point by boating an 835-pounder on the *Lourdes*. Long Islander Richie Koch caught an 875-pounder that same month on his *Libra*, after having boated a 900-pounder the previous year.

Capt. Len Belcaro, whose Offshore Services in Manasquan, New Jersey, distributes ocean-temperature charts, spotted a huge temperature break in Spencer Canyon during September, and rounded up a charter party to run out there on his *Midnight Express* from Point Pleasant. After Belcaro crossed the line from green 68.9-degree water to blue 77.8-degree water, Bob Cole of Easton, Maryland, hooked a 756-pound blue. An 852-pounder had been boated by a Long Island boat in Hudson Canyon earlier that month.

Warm blue water of 75 degrees or more seems to be one of the keys to catching blue marlin in the northern canyons, but there are always exceptions. A big one occurred on September 30, when the *Sea Sons* was trolling for tuna at the Texas Tower (about 15 miles inshore of Hudson Canyon) and Buddy Pinkava of Springfield, New Jersey, released an estimated 700-pound blue that hit in 64-degree waters.

New Tactics Needed

The fact that fair numbers of blue marlin are being caught in northern canyons indicates there may be more of these fish around than anglers suspect. The fact of the matter is that almost no one is specifically targeting them. Practically all are caught incidentally while fishing for tunas or white marlin. The same baits and lures that attract those species will often interest blues, but I've rarely heard of anyone using techniques aimed just at blues. For instance, Florida and Venezuela skippers often slow-troll live little tunny (false albacore) for blues, yet northern canyon fishermen rarely use live bait for trolling. Even if little tunny aren't available that far offshore, skipjacks often are, and chicken dolphin can be caught around most any lobster pot buoy.

Lures Work Best

Almost every notable blue taken in the northern canyons has fallen for a high-speed lure. The *Tempo's* 1,174-pounder hit one of Clemenz's 14-inch Kona-type lures, while a dark-blue/light-blue Kona-head caught Infantolino's 1,046-pounder. Santoro's big blue took an R&S with a pearl head and pink-and-white skirt, and Belcaro scored with a Mold Craft Soft Head in pink and white, fished behind by three birds. On the other hand, many of the tournament blues did hit bait, and the *Dulcinea's* big winner last August grabbed a skirted ballyhoo.

Although South Jersey canyon fishermen regularly fish the 500- and 1,000-fathom lines of the canyons because they aren't much farther offshore than the 100-fathom line, that doesn't apply to the north. Would more Hudson Canyon blues be hooked if similar attention were paid to the deeper offshore drops, which are rarely fished by anyone other than long-liners?

I don't have the answers, and it may be years before we know just how good the northern blue marlin fishery might be. It certainly isn't close to shore, as it is with many blue marlin hot spots around the world, and it will take some dedication (and money) to run the extra miles and fish with methods that won't provide the variety action canyon anglers have become used to. All we can say at this point is that the fishery has been improving and that the effort to target blue marlin could pay off with some big catches!

Jigging the Tailers

by Jim Hendricks

What do you do when tailing striped marlin turn up their noses at live baits? Jig 'em!

They were the best of conditions. They were the worst of conditions. For marlin fishing, that is.

Seas off the East Cape of Mexico's Baja California were flat-calm, tabletop conditions. "Greased out" is the way we Californians describe it.

The water was great for boating, but bad for marlin fishing. Striped marlin in particular do not bite well without some sort of wave action. It seems to get them stirred up and ready to feed on the surface.

And yet on this windless day in May on the lower Sea of Cortez, the marlin were around. You could see them, the tall, slender upper half of each tail slicing the flat ocean surface as they cruised along in groups of three, five, seven or more.

Presently, Phil Troy – longtime fishing friend and *SWS* staff member – spotted another group of tailing marlin through his binoculars, about 300 yards off our starboard beam. Our skipper, Ramon, swung the wheel over hard and punched the throttle ahead to intercept the fish. Meanwhile, we prepared live mackerel to cast once we were within tossing distance to the marlin.

This is a well-rehearsed drill that has become standard operating procedure among marlin fishermen in both Baja and Southern California. Instead of hoping the fish bite the trolling lures (we call them "marlin jigs" on the West Coast), a live bait such as a mackerel or scad (known as a "caballito" in Mexico) is presented instead.

As Ramon spurred the 26-foot sportfisherman into position, two live baits went sailing to starboard, landing perfectly ten to 15 feet in front of the tailing marlin. "Bueno!" Ramon yelled from the flying bridge.

The fish disappeared below the surface and we braced ourselves for the strike. But nothing happened. "What gives?" Phil asked, the question reflecting everyone's bewilderment.

Suddenly the fish popped up again, this time off our starboard bow. "Reel! Reel!" came the excited orders from the bridge, as Ramon punched the single diesel again. We quickly caught up and once again presented the lively mackerel to the fish. And just as before, we were ignored. The fish sunk away and never reappeared.

Had this been the first time we'd been shunned, the experience might not have held much significance. But it was the third shut-out in three tries on the same day. It was clear that a trend was developing.

The dead-calm conditions certainly seemed to be a factor. Whatever the case, conventional West Coast marlin wisdom was not producing. Ramon recognized the need to change tactics.

The language barrier prevented the skipper from describing in detail what he had in mind, so it was not until we gunned ahead toward another group of tailing marlin that we learned about the change in plans.

"No, no!" came the command from above, just as we were getting ready to cast. "Un momento!" yelled Ramon over the noise of the revving diesel. Standing at the wheel, his eyes were transfixed on the tailing fish. Phil and I glanced up, glanced at each other, and shrugged. Instead of presenting live baits, Ramon wanted to pull the marlin jigs at high speed past the tailing marlin. "An odd choice," I thought, since I'd been trained in the school of live-bait fishing since I began marlin fishing over ten years ago.

The boat sped ahead of the fish and Ramon brought her about hard, placing the jigs directly in front of the tailers. The fish lit up and came charging, to my utter amazement. Before we could even drop back a bait, one of the fish inhaled a jig and we were hooked up solid.

Grant's First Fish

Phil and I both brought our youngest sons (Phil's son Joe is 13 while my son Grant is ten) on this trip. Since Grant had never caught a marlin before, it was his turn on the rod and reel. For a ten-year-old, he did an admirable job. The fish was boatside within 35 minutes. After a tagging job and a few photos, we released the fish – a striped marlin estimated at 140 pounds.

We went on that day and the next to hook six more marlin. The conditions remained the same – dead calm. And the technique that produced the hookups from the tailing marlin was Ramon's method, a routine we came to call "jiggin' 'em."

Not all of the tailers bit the jigs. But once they became interested in the lures we dropped back live mackerel. And in their excited state, they willingly ate. Yet we found the tailers would not eat unless the jigs were presented to whet their appetites.

At the end of two days, I was more curious than ever about this technique, and so I sought out someone who could expand on the rationale and method. After asking around, I ran across Jesus "Chuy" Valdez, general manager of the Hotel Buena Vista, a newly renovated beach and sportfishing resort nestled on the sweeping, picturesque coast of the Cabo's East Cape.

Valdez has fished this region nearly all of his years, and has a deep affection for the land, sea, and life of this rugged area. While he rarely takes guests fishing himself anymore, he still personally manages the Hotel Buena Vista sportfishing fleet and knows almost instinctively what it takes to catch fish.

Valdez confirmed that the calm conditions have an influence on the tactics used on tailing marlin. But he also said that the technique Ramon showed us would work equally well when the seas are running larger.

"We found long ago down here that we have to be flexible in our thinking and sport fishing techniques," Valdez explained. "We have to do everything possible to help our guests catch fish, and that means being able to adapt to conditions and the fish's feeding behavior.

"Many anglers – experienced sport fishermen – think that a tailing marlin can't resist a well-presented live bait. Yet I've seen them turn up their bills and swim away hundreds of times.

"So we got to thinking: 'What could we do to get them interested in eating?' Out of frustration more than anything else, we started driving the boat right in front the fish, letting the lures run almost over their heads. It worked."

Engine Noise a Factor

"I think it's the churning of the propeller, the boat's wake and all the commotion that gets them excited," said Valdez. "It must simulate feeding activity. And then the trolling lures come along, looking like a baitfish trying to get away."

What about once the fish get excited? Should you let the fish eat the jigs or go ahead and present a live bait?

According to Valdez, dropping back a live bait is still the preferred method for hooking marlin when using the "jig 'em" technique.

"Once the fish are excited, our skippers will often speed the boat up or troll lines in closer to the boat," said Valdez. "The object is to keep the marlin from striking the trolling lures, yet keep them interested while a live bait is dropped back to the fish."

"We find that more marlin stay hooked when they take a live bait than when they take a trolling lure. But when the tailing marlin get fussy, we can't hook them on live bait unless we have the lures out to get them excited."

It Works in California

The technique we learned from the experts at Hotel Buena Vista proved to be just as sound on tailing marlin off Southern California, as I was to learn on another trip closer to home.

It was a sloppy August day atop the Osborne Bank near Santa Barbara Island, with southeast winds shoving steep seas up to eight feet over the submarine mount. The striped marlin were thick on the Osborne – tailing once again. And just as on those two days off the East Cape, the conventional methods weren't working. We had cast live baits to at least six groups of tailers without even a hint of interest.

We had just returned to trolling after yet another unsuccessful attempt when it all came back to me. Of course, it was nearly the same situation as on the East Cape. Instantly, I knew what to do.

Moments later, we spotted another group of tailers. We turned the boat upsea to intercept the fish. As the jigs and white water swept over the fish, the marlin sank away and so did my heart. "This is not going to work here," I thought.

But I was wrong. Within seconds, one marlin broke ranks and began chasing the jigs – agitated, aggressive and illuminated with radiating bars of purple.

Barely conscious of my steps, I bounded from bridge to cockpit and lobbed a live mackerel into the prop wash. When the mackerel reached the marlin, the water literally exploded. I fed line as the spool whirled at high speed below my fingertips. I counted … one, two, three and four, then I threw the reel into gear and set the hook hard three times.

Hooked solid, the fish staged an aerial show that would put the Blue Angels to shame. Within 30 minutes, we tagged and released the spent marlin. As we watched the tired striper swim away, I silently thanked Ramon – the man who first showed me how to turn a tailing marlin from coy to crazy just by "jiggin' 'em."

BILLFISH:

White Gold

by John Cacciutti

White marlin tournament champs share their secrets for bringing home the big bucks.

Make no bones about it, winning a white marlin tournament is not easy money. It takes a crew working together like a well-oiled machine, days of preparation, painstaking attention to detail, and a captain with enough salt on the brain to find fish intuitively. Even so, this is not a magic formula for success, as white marlin have been known to make monkeys out of mavens.

Legendary white marlin fisherman Captain Fred Riffe won the Ocean City (Maryland) Marlin Club white marlin tag-and-release award seven years in a row, yet once missed hooking the same fish 17 times! Dick Weber, owner of the *South Jersey Champion*, has actively pursued whites for more than 30 years and is respected as one of New Jersey's all-time best white marlin fishermen, yet he considers a 40- to 50-percent hookup ratio excellent.

So, what can be done to improve your chances when there's big money on the line? We probed the minds of various white marlin authorities, including oceanographers and tournament champions, to find out.

Where the Fish Are

When it comes to locating whites for tournaments along the East Coast, at least half the battle is finding the prime trolling territory. White marlin are traditionally sought after in depths between 30 and 500 fathoms, but other factors are involved in where they'll be.

Len Belcaro of Offshore Satellite Services, the hometown sea-temperature charting company in the Northeast, regards white marlin as "opportunistic feeders." He explains: "No matter how deep the water may be, as long as there's a good temperature break holding bait, white marlin will visit and return to the site." To illustrate, Belcaro confides that most of the billfish caught in the 1995 Mid-Atlantic $500,000 Tournament came from a thin, warm-water finger beyond the 1,000-fathom line, yet he also recalled a year when anglers were getting 20 to 30 shots a day at white marlin in just 19 fathoms.

Captain Tom Henry of the Ocean City charter boat *Waterdog* says he spends a lot of time fishing inside the 100-fathom line. Henry took home more than $258,000 at the Mid-Atlantic $500,000 Tournament. "Wherever I find a temperature break, good water color and bait, I concentrate my efforts – even if it means staying within a two-mile area all day," Henry explained. In shallow water, diverse bottom structure like the 40-Fathom Fingers that coincides with a temperature break is where bait and game fish will congregate. Canyon fishermen who overshoot these areas often pass up large concentrations of whites.

In water beyond 100 fathoms, which is favored by blue marlin, bottom structure is of diminishing value. Here the prudent billfisherman must rely principally on temperature changes and surface signs, such as weedlines, bait schools and slicks. With this in mind, it's easy to see why sea-surface temperature charts or fishing reports less than a day old are paramount to success. Winners simply don't leave the dock blind.

Hooking up with Naturals

White marlin may be more difficult to hook than other billfish, but according to the marine biologists I queried, their mouths aren't any harder. The difference is that blue marlin feed like aggressive pit bulls, while whites spend more time "window shopping" before they bite.

The majority of pros surveyed fish mostly natural baits or "combination" baits (naturals dressed with small lures or skirts). Some feel that artificials are genuinely boring, since the reels are fished in strike drag and the fish basically hooks itself. "Natural baits promote more of a personal contest between angler and fish," Weber explains. "With naturals, the angler has to practically hand-feed the marlin and then make a decision to set the hook at just the right time."

Most experts also believe a missed fish will return to a natural bait more often than to an artificial. Bally-hoo are the most popular bait, followed by swimming mullet and eels. Captain Henry fishes naked baits exclusively, while most others dress at least some of their ballyhoo with a Sea Witch, Tournament Tackle Tracker, or some other small lure to add action, bubbles and color to the spread. William Pope, winner of the Cape Fear Blue Water Fishing Club Release Award in 1995 and runner-up in 1996, favors a Hatteras Lure Chaser rig, which has also been an outstanding producer on my *Marathon John*.

This daisy-chain-type rig features five tiny Mylar® skirts spaced 12 inches apart on a leader with a bally-hoo and Sea Dart lure combination at the end. The highly-reflective skirts simulate frightened baitfish "lighting up" as if they were fleeing the ballyhoo hot on their tail. The chase scene sparks the predatory instinct in marlin and other game fish.

Small-to-medium-sized ballyhoo are the universal preference among seasoned white marlin tournament players, and most allow about a five second dropback before setting the hook. If the fish drops the bait, they reel quickly and often get another bite. The *South Jersey Champion* crew is one of the few that allows only a short dropback of two to five seconds.

Weber believes that too long of a dropback is much worse than one that is too short. "A fish that feels the hook or senses resistance on the line is less likely to return than one that believes the bait successfully evaded its bite," he explains. "A short dropback will keep the fish within sight of the spread, allowing it several baits to choose from if it misses the first."

One thread of advice that everyone agreed on was to hit the fish any time you notice its head turned, because the best time to strike a marlin is when the line is at a right angle to the jaw.

Understanding Lures

Practically every offshore lure known to man has caught white marlin at one time or another. Those skippers who prefer lures, like Captain Herb Schoenberg of the *Harry II*, another winner of the prestigious Mid-Atlantic $500,000 Tournament and the Ocean City Marlin and Tuna Club Overnight Tournament, endorse a variety, but certain features stand out. Soft-head lures, such as those made by Mold Craft and Sevenstrand, are preferred for their ability to produce repeated strikes, and the highly reflective Mylar® skirt material used by Hatteras and the Bob Schneider Lure Company also drew applause. Favorite colors may be easiest to remember as black-and-something: black-and-purple, black-and-orange, and black-and-pink were repeated again and again. Lure shapes prove important as well. Jetheads and chuggers are popular, but erratic swimmers are usually avoided.

To spice up a straight-running natural-bait spread and provide at least one sizeable offering for a blue marlin, many captains troll a single large lure, long and down the middle. My all-time favorite for this is a black-and-orange metallic lure with a very uncommon head shape, given to me by Captain Bob Paulson of the charter boat *Prowler* in Key West, Florida. It swims slightly, but not enough to frustrate a pursuing marlin. I've caught more white and blue marlin, huge wahoo, and dolphin on that lure than all other lures combined. Hatteras Lure Company is now manufacturing a nearly identical lure with the highly reflective skirts mentioned earlier.

Regardless of what kind of lure is trolled, reels should always be set at strike drag. There is no dropback when fishing artificials. In fact, professionals emphasize the need for tag lines to further reduce dropback time. The ideal hookup with artificials occurs on the initial strike. Schoenberg uses tag lines tied directly to the 'rigger poles and substitutes No. 64 rubber bands for release clips. "When the fish hits, I want the hook to set immediately," he says. "With the tag lines tied directly to the 'riggers, there is no give, and it takes approximately 20 pounds of pressure to break the rubber band."

A 7/0 or 8/0 hook rigged on an 80- to 100-pound mono leader was unanimously preferred by the experts for white marlin fishing. Tackle selection ranged from 20- to 50-pound test, with Shimano TLD 25s being the reels most often mentioned.

As for teasers, the majority of experts use an artificial squid chain on one side and a chain of swimming mullet or ballyhoo on the other. Several captains raved about the Hatteras Lures Ultimate Teaser – a pair of lures and a bird rigged to simulate two fish competing for bait. "I see a lot of fish come in on that teaser," Pope says. "It seems to get things started, even when other boats around me aren't catching."

When pulling teasers, it's imperative to have a small ballyhoo hooked up to a 20-pound outfit that's ready to deploy at a moment's notice. If a marlin comes up on the teaser, the mate pulls the teaser away while an angler simultaneously feeds out the small bait on the light outfit. Of the experts polled, those with the most crowded trophy shelves report catching most of their fish in this fashion.

The bottom line is that it's a lot easier to hook whites on light tackle, so you'd better give up the big gear – or you could spend a lot of green trying to strike gold!

Tournament Checklist

1. Rigging needle, waxed line and ballyhoo wire; rubber bands.

2. Teasers, lures, bait, ice and salt.

3. Sharpened 7/0 or 8/0 hooks.

4. Mono leader (80- to 130-pound test).

5. Ball-bearing snap swivels, crimps and crimping tool.

6. Knives and pliers.

7. Grease pencil (near radio), navigation charts and water-temperature chart.

8. Polarizing sunglasses (for everyone).

9. Tagging stick and tags.

10. Sharpened flying gaff, large and small straight gaff.

11. Load new line on reels.

12. Set and test drags with scale.

13. Lubricate roller guides.

14. Check leader knots and crimps.

15. Teach everyone onboard what you want them to do when you get a strike and when you hook up. Show them what to look for and let them help you find the fish.

16. Set out the equipment that may be needed in a hurry (i.e., harness, gimbel belt, gloves, gaff, tail rope, etc.).

Sailfishing with the Pros

by John Brownlee

*Three top South Florida charter captains reveal
how they score with sailfish, day after day.*

During the last few winters, Southeast Florida experienced some of its best sailfish action in recent memory, especially off Palm Beach. The last two weeks of January saw many boats returning to the dock with double-digit release flags flying from their outrigger halyards, and five-fish days were being called "average." During the winter Buccaneer Tournament in 1996, some 35 boats released over 600 sails in three days.

Almost all of the skippers fishing out of Palm Beach use live bait these days, although there are still a few tournaments that don't allow it. In fact, there are some people who feel that the proliferation of live-bait fishing has made sailfishing too easy. Indeed, when the sails are biting fast and furious, it can be hard to miss when you're fishing a spread of lively goggle-eyes.

But there are many more days when the action isn't fast and furious, and this is when the pros delve into their bag of tricks to make things happen. We recently caught up with three of South Florida's top charter captains to get some tips on what they do to catch sailfish day after day, even when the action's slow. Here's what they had to say:

Capt. Jim Garner

All three of the captains we spoke with talked about the importance of "reading" the water to give you a clue as to where to set up and fish. Capt. Jim Garner, who runs the 51-foot *Major Motion* out of Sailfish Marina in Palm Beach Shores, says you have to be able to predict where the fish will be.

"We look for all of the usual signs," Garner explains, "things like working birds, surface rips, and temperature or color changes. With rips, you need to find out which way the current is running and fish on one side or the other."

"Sailfish travel with the wind and water temperature," he continued. "That's why a strong north wind tends to bring them down to us here in the Palm Beaches. At night, they settle down and move back to the north again. The body of fish can go by you real fast, and that's why the action might get red hot all of a sudden after being slow for hours."

Garner says moon phase is important, too, with the week leading up to the full moon being the time when the sails feed most heavily. After the full moon passes, he feels the fish tend to scatter and don't eat as well.

The *Major Motion* crew prefers live bait, usually goggle-eyes or tinker mackerel, and sets a spread of four rigger lines and sometimes a fifth flat line.

As for tackle, Garner prefers conventional over spinning gear, saying that conventional reels are better when backing down on a fish. "We fish 20-pound test on Penn International 30s and Shimano TLD 25s," he explains. "Spinning gear just doesn't have enough line capacity when you have multiple hookups and you have to let one fish run while you chase another. Spinners also don't take up line fast enough. With the high gear ratios and large spools of the conventional reels, you can gain line very quickly while backing down."

Capt. George LaBonte

George LaBonte, who runs the charter boat *Grand Slam* out of Jupiter Inlet, is a live-bait expert. The *Grand Slam* is a Boca Grande center console, which offers more of a "hands-on" charter experience

for those who want to learn more about sailfishing firsthand.

LaBonte catches all of his own live bait, which means his day starts early, long before sunrise. "My standard program centers on live bait," LaBonte says. "I focus on getting a large quantity of bait. While most boats leave the dock with one or two dozen baits, I usually have 10 to 12 dozen goggle-eyes in the well before heading offshore."

With that many fresh baits available, LaBonte can afford to change his baits frequently. "I switch baits every ten minutes," he explains. "I start at the left side and change the rigger, then the flat. Then I move to the right side and repeat the process. This way I always have a few hot baits in the water, since they are always most frantic when they are first put out, and that really turns the sailfish on!" LaBonte also likes to keep a couple of pitch baits ready, in case a sail swims by, near the surface.

Having a lot of bait is the cornerstone of Labonte's sailfishing philosophy, but where to fish is obviously of great importance as well. On this point he makes an interesting note. "Many times we have been in shallow water, 50 to 75 feet deep, trying to catch bait like cigar minnows and tinker mackerel when goggle-eyes were tough to find, and have had sailfish pop up right next to the boat. I started thinking, 'Why run out to 200 feet when we know the fish are here?' Indeed, the best fishing in the last couple of years seems to have occurred inshore, on top of bait schools in 75 to 100 feet of water.

Incidentally, LaBonte uses Sabiki rigs (right) to catch cigar minnows and mackerel, hanging six to ten ounces of lead under the rig to keep the hooks from tangling on the way down.

When rigging his sailfish baits, LaBonte prefers 50-pound-test leader with a short wire trace at the end in case a wahoo shows up. He also uses razor-sharp Owner hooks. "You don't even have to set the hook with Owners," he says. "Just wind until the line is tight and the fish will be on solid."

LaBonte doesn't really like kites, although he will sometimes fly one off the bow. Instead, he generally fishes all his baits from the riggers. "Most guys who fish out here a lot don't really believe you get more bites on a kite," LaBonte says. "The sailfish bite the rigger baits just fine, but the key is to position them correctly and then move them as little as possible. The main thing is getting over the schools of bait."

Capt. Chip Shafer

Chip Shafer divides his time between Manteo, North Carolina, where he charters during the summer, and Fort Pierce, Florida, where you can find him each winter. He also makes a springtime detour to Mexico to fish for sailfish and other species. Shafer is one of those guys who feels that too many boats are fishing with live bait, making it "too easy" to catch a sail. Consequently, he only fishes with rigged dead bait aboard his 53-foot *Temptress*.

"Live bait is so good it makes the game easier than it needs to be," says Shafer, who also believes that the use of live bait is more harmful to the fish. "When a bunch of boats are live-baiting," he says, "and these incredible numbers of fish are being caught, it seems like we must be the single biggest

threat to the health of sailfish in the area."

Shafer prefers to troll for sails, and ballyhoo is his bait of choice, the smaller the better. "We like 16-count ballyhoo, which is 16 dozen to a case," he says. Shafer's crew normally fishes six lines: two long riggers, two short riggers and two flat lines. Naked ballyhoo are fished on four of the lines. A fifth line pulls a ballyhoo with a small blue-and-white Sea Witch skirt. Finally, a strip bait with a Sea Witch skirt is fished off a rigger. In front of the flat lines, Shafer runs a spreader-bar teaser rigged with fresh mullet to attract the sails.

"We use 80-pound Jinkai leader with Mustad 9175 hooks, from 5/0 to 7/0, depending on the size of the bait," Shafer says. "I know a lot of guys use lighter leaders and fancier hooks, but I don't feel you need it. They bite on that Jinkai real good."

Shafer likes to fish in water between 80 and 250 feet deep, claiming that 75 percent of the sails are caught in water between 120 and 180 feet deep. "We look for decent water in that depth range, and we usually start off with what worked yesterday," he explained.

"Another important factor in sailfishing is the radio. Don't be afraid to use it. You should have a group of people you can put stock in for information, and be ready to change your plan if you hear the bite is happening somewhere else. In addition, you shouldn't hesitate to tell others if you are getting the bites."

BILLFISH:
Slick Tricks for Sails

by George Poveromo

If you're new to Florida sailfishing, or just want to increase your catch, try these simple, effective techniques.

If you didn't like fishing, this would seem truly crazy. That's what I was thinking one brutally cold morning while Mark Cellura and I unhooked goggle-eyes from our quill rigs. It was 5:00 A.M. and quite dark. A northwest wind was driving a chill through our bodies, making three layers of clothing and foul-weather gear seem inadequate. Every now and then a light would go on in one of the ocean-front condos. And while we couldn't see the individuals inside, just the thought of them sipping coffee made us envious.

Fortunately, we were able to round up about five

dozen baits before sunrise. We sped along the beach, heading several miles north of Lake Worth Inlet, before turning offshore. The farther we ran from the beach, the lumpier the seas became. Then, in 160 feet of water, we noticed a defined rip with lots of flying fish activity.

We began our drift in five-foot seas, pitching out live baits. Mark and I were freelining two small flat-line baits when they were picked up in rapid succession. Mark struck first; I set up seconds later. As expected, two sailfish danced through the whitecaps.

By day's end, we had tallied eight releases. It was a typical sailfish day where you weathered the cold and took your share of lumps and bruises. Yes, indeed – if you didn't like fishing, it would seem like pure hell.

Sailfish Signs

South Florida's sailfish action is at its best in winter and spring. And although just about anyone might be able to catch a fish or two on live bait, running up big numbers demands some refined techniques. One of the biggest keys is locating a concentration of fish. You'll most likely find the fish in 90 to 250 feet of water. Within this zone, look for sharp, well-defined color changes, rips and bait activity. The latter includes diving birds and showering flying fish, as well as any bait concentrations picked up on the sonar. A satellite water-temperature chart, like those provided by Roffer's Ocean Fishing Forecasting Service in Miami, can show you the precise locations of currents and warm-water eddies from the Gulf Stream. Both bait and gamefish often congregate along the edges of such currents.

One way of locating fish is to establish a shallow-to-deep drifting or slow trolling pattern. For instance, if the wind is blowing from the northwest, I'll shutdown in 80 feet of water, letting the wind and seas push the boat offshore into 250 feet of water. Conversely, if the wind is out of the east or northeast, I'll set up in 250 feet of water and begin drifting inshore.

Sailfish often travel in pods. If you raise a fish, take note of the depth and store the coordinates in the loran or GPS; you'll want to concentrate on that specific pocket of water. On occasion, persistent west or northwest breezes push clean water and fish out into the 500- and 600-foot depths. Conversely, strong easterly winds often push clean water closer to shore. So don't be afraid of fishing deeper or shallower if conditions warrant. Remember, locate the bait and the sails should be around.

Best Baits

The best sailfish baits are usually the smallest. Goggle-eyes are good kite baits because they are hearty. However, herring and pilchards are outstanding flat-line baits, followed by small goggle-eyes, runners and mullet. Herring and pilchards are small enough for a sailfish to easily consume.

Plus, their soft texture enables a hook to easily tear free and lodge in the fish's mouth. Your hookup rate will undoubtedly rise if you use these baits.

To maximize your bait's ability to swim, while reducing the terminal hardware that might be visible to sailfish, use 3/0 and 4/0 hooks on herring and pilchards (Eagle Claw #250 or Mustad 92671) and no larger than a 5/0 hook on goggle-eyes, runners and mullet. Hook the herring and pilchards just in front of the dorsal fin for kite and flat-line use. Hook goggle-eyes, runners and mullet the same way, or above the anal fin if you want them to swim deep on flat lines. Use a monofilament leader no heavier than 50-pound test, scaling down to 30-pound-test on 12-pound-test tackle or when strikes are hard to come by. I generally tie a short Bimini twist in my fishing line, followed by a small barrel swivel to prevent line twist. Finally, I add a 12-foot leader to the swivel's opposite eye.

A GOGGLE-EYE rigged for kite fishing.

Setting the Spread

I prefer still-drifting, which enables the baits to swim more naturally. With a small crew I'll fish two baits off the kite and three baits off the opposite gunwale. As mentioned, small to medium-sized baits are fished on the kites. On the flat lines, one outfit is fished with a balloon float fished about a foot above the leader, which keeps the bait within 12 feet of the surface. One bait is free-lined without a float, while the third flat-line is set at about 90 feet on a downrigger.

A "TRIGGER" made from soft wire allows the line to freespool on the strike.

The two surface flat lines, usually 20-pound spinning outfits, are fished with open bails. The line is held in place with a "trigger" made of soft rigging wire. When a fish eats, the wire bends, releasing and freespooling the line. The angler grabs the

rod, closes the bail and sets the hook. The downrigger is set fairly loosely; that way, a fish feels minimal resistance when it eats the bait. The slack line between the strike and the actual hookup is often enough for a sufficient drop-back on the downrigger, so the bail on the downrigger rod is left closed.

Keep 'Em Kicking

The kite baits warrant the most attention. Because wind velocities vary, you'll have to continually fine-tune the baits. Each bait's dorsal should barely break the surface, so it creates a distressed splashing sound. When the wind increases the kite rises and lifts the bait from the water. When the wind decreases the kite falls some and the baits descend below the surface. I prefer 20-pound-test conventional outfits on the kites, which makes it quicker and easier to adjust the baits.

On the strike, give the fish only a second or two to get the bait in its mouth, then engage the drag and reel quickly. The pull of the fish taking off line should trip the kite clip. Continue taking in the slack until the fish begins pulling against the drag, then set up.

During the fight, keep an eye on the remaining lines, removing only those that might interfere with the hooked fish. Sails often travel in groups, and you'll have an excellent chance at a double- or even triple-header by leaving those baits in place. If the action slows consider slow-trolling back to the area where you had the last strike.

Challenge of the Broadbill

by Capt. Mike "Beak" Hurt

The calm, temperate waters off Southern California are considered some of the best in the world to catch the ultimate challenge in big-game fishing – the broadbill swordfish.

Catching a swordfish on rod and reel has never been easy. The chances of seeing one are slim, coaxing them to eat is difficult, and the odds of landing the fish if you are lucky enough to hook up are lower than for any other big-game fish. Zane Grey, in his *Adventures of a Deep Sea Angler,* first published in 1930, logs the task of fishing for broadbill off Catalina one summer: "In 67 days I ran 3,450 miles, I saw 79 broadbill swordfish, had 12 strikes and caught 7 fish."

You may think working that hard for a fish isn't worth the effort – but that's precisely why it's such a big deal to catch a swordfish. And while entry into the prestigious "rod-and-reel swordfish club" isn't

getting any easier, there have been good showings of these fish off Southern California in the last few years. The key is being prepared for a chance encounter when you're cruising offshore.

There are two main methods of rod-and-reel swordfishing: daytime sight fishing and nighttime drift fishing. Although the swordfish's feeding habits are primarily nocturnal, most of the West Coast fish are caught during the day via the former approach.

When sight fishing, you must seek, spot and present the bait to the fish. It's a hunter's dream. Most fish are spotted while the boat is trolling at higher speeds for tuna or marlin. In fact, one of the advantages of looking for fish at faster trolling speeds is that you can cover more water. Once you find an area that has a few fish around, work it carefully. Ideally, you want to slow down to five or six knots, which allows you to study the water more thoroughly.

A good pair of binoculars and the knowledge of how to use them are a must. A "high and dry" fish will have its distinctive fins sticking proudly in the air as it cruises briefly on the surface. Many novice off-shore fishermen may confuse a sleeping marlin that raises its dorsal, or a large shark swimming along just beneath the surface, for a swordfish. Even seals sunning themselves while floating on the surface with their fins sticking straight up have momentarily excited anxious anglers. But once you've seen the real thing, you'll never make the mistake again. With time, a good spotter can tell it's a sword by the wake it creates as it swims along. The wide, swinging bill and the motion of its rigid, forked tail fin give them away to the trained eye. The action of the tail is very different from that of a blue shark, for instance, which flops from side to side. That's because the tail section of the sword's backbone is fused. It takes concentration and practice to become a good spotter, and, as in any form of sight fishing, the more eyes scanning the water, the better.

Searching for Swords

The best time of year to look for swords is when the surface temperature is between the low 60s and the mid-70s. The best time of day is during a midday slack tide, but I've seen them at all hours. I know I've even run over them at night by noticing the phosphorescent trail they leave in the water.

When targeting swordfish, choose an area based on previous information, signs or known haunts, and arrive at least an hour before the slack tide. Once you do find a fish, there are two basic ways to present your bait.

Trolling a rigged, dead bait is very popular. Squid is considered swordfish candy, but tuna, bonito, mackerel, flying fish and other indigenous pelagic baits are fine. Simply put, swordfish will eat what's available. In fact, I once cleaned a swordfish that had two cormorants in its stomach! If you can get your hands on some hake, a bottom fish that swords love to slurp down while feeding at night, give that a try. To cover your bet you should carry an assortment of both fresh and frozen baits.

Swords Off the Bow!

Once a sword is spotted, there's usually a mad scramble in the boat. However, a discussed or practiced plan of attack will help eliminate confusion. This is no time for stupid mistakes. First, note the behavior of the fish – how it's swimming and which way it's heading. Approach with caution, slowly and quietly. When you're close to the fish, drop the bait back 100 yards or so (depending on the size of the boat and color of the water) while idling around the finning fish.

Be ready! Swordfish can strike like no other fish. I've had them hit the bait so hard with their huge bill that 80-pound monofilament reacted like a snapped rubber band as the strike was transmitted up the line. Other times the fish has taken off so fast (usually after being spooked by the leader) that it was all I could do to keep the reel from backlashing.

Swordfish are not only strong; they are quite capable of blistering speed and snap reactions. One technique that helps prevent mishaps on the strike is to free-spool lots of line in the water. This gives the fish more time to eat the bait without interruption from an excited angler using too much thumb pressure.

Live-Bait Tactics

When trolling live bait, the technique is much the same, except that you need to be able to control the behavior of the bait. You want it to swim down as it's being presented, since my experience has taught me that swords aren't able to see well straight ahead or upward. A dead bait is easy to sink compared to a freaked-out livey that has its motor running at full throttle, trying to escape the arena into which it has been tossed. Clipping the tail of a strong bait helps to keep it on the dinner table longer. Also, I like to hook the bait in the back rather than through the nose. This hook position helps persuade the bait to swim down and away from the boat. A nose-hooked bait tends to stay on the surface. Baits also have trouble towing the large hook and heavy line by the nose, and will often circle back to the boat.

A single hook should be used so the bait can swim more naturally, while a double-hook rig is preferred with a dead bait. A lot of fish caught are actually foul-hooked, so stronger, forged big game hooks are preferred over the lighter bait hooks commonly used for striped marlin. Always make sure the hook is correctly sharpened; however, the point can't be

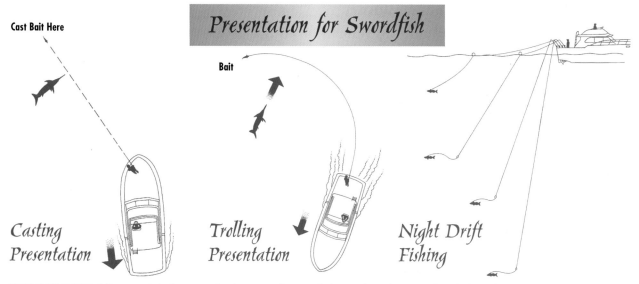

Cast Bait Here

Bait

Presentation for Swordfish

Casting Presentation

Trolling Presentation

Night Drift Fishing

WHEN SIGHT CASTING (left), approach the finning sword with caution and position the boat so the angler can cast from the bow. Place the live bait ahead of, and outside the fish. This discourages the surprised bait from trying to run back under the boat, as it'll have to pass in front of the swordfish. Back away briefly while free spooling line to put more distance between you and the bait. (center) Drop a trolled bait back far enough behind the boat so you can maneuver around the finning fish without spooking it. Troll the bait while circling the fish. When the bait is in position where you think the swordfish can see it, stop the boat and free-spool the line, allowing it to swim or sink down. When the fish moves on the bait, dump more line in the water and prepare for a blistering run. (right) Cover as much of the water column as you can when drifting at night. The closest bait has the most weight for the deepest presentation, and the farthest bait out has none at all. Floats are used to position the baits at varying depths and distances from the boat.

too thin or it will bend when it comes in contact with the sword's tough skin.

Whether you use live or dead bait, long, heavy leaders are required. The swordfish's bill is a coarse double-edged blade that I've seen cut a mako shark in half with one quick whack. Swords have a tendency to get tangled in the leader when attacking the bait, so you need extra length. Thirty feet of 250- to 400-pound leader attached to a matching ball-bearing snap swivel allows for quick and easy bait changing. Last season I had good success with fluorocarbon, which is much less visible in the water than regular monofilament. It also sinks faster than other lines due to its higher specific gravity.

Casting Call

Another popular method of baiting a swordfish is casting a live bait off the bow, as is often done with striped marlin. A big proponent of this method is one of the most respected fishermen on the West Coast, Capt. Gene Grimes, who is constantly coming up with new ways of catching fish. In 1978 Grimes proved that casting live baits (he likes large mackerel) was the most productive way to catch the elusive broadbill. Grimes and his team on the *Legend* weighed in a record 11 swords that season!

This method takes an experienced angler, however, since heavy tackle is preferred. Large rod guides are required to accommodate the 80-pound line and 250-pound leader. The leader is usually connected to the main line via a wind-on leader knot, such as an albright, blood or uni-knot. Lighter line may get down a bit better, but you're in for a long tug of war. Three years ago, a 213-pound fish was landed on 30-pound gear after an exhausting 24-hour battle.

A live mackerel is the mainstay for casting, and the larger the bait the bigger the hook you can use. Approach the fish as you would a "sleeper" marlin if the swordfish is milling in a characteristic circle. Sometimes they seem to be going somewhere and are traveling in a straight line. In this case, you have to maneuver the boat ahead of the fish and cast as it approaches.

Either way, one of the tricks used by Capt. Grimes is to back away slowly after the cast is made, because you don't want the bait to run under the boat for protection. Depending on the situation, I've punched the throttles momentarily while backing away, not only to push the bait away but also to get the attention of this curious game fish. (I feel that the circle of bubbles created by the props resembles a bait ball.) After the presentation, feed line into the water as mentioned above, and wait for the fish to pick up the bait.

If the fish dives, don't move until you relocate it. Work the area, especially upcurrent of where you last saw the fish, since it may resurface later. There's also a good chance of finding another fish in close proximity. Although largely considered an independent fish, swords do group together in a spread-out fashion of schooling. I've never seen them schooled up like marlin, but I have encountered numerous fish in a relatively small area.

Night Moves for Swords?

According to research, swordfish prefer to feed at night. Drift fishing at night became an internationally recognized method due to some great success by anglers in Florida in the 1970s, and has made entrance into the "club" more accessible since then.

Grimes, along with fellow captain Kenny Dickerson, proved in 1975 that it could be done off California. There have been a few caught at night in our waters since then, but it's still not as popular a technique as baiting individual fish in the daytime. Some say there aren't enough fish around to make it worthwhile, but I know that gillnet boats fishing in front of Newport Beach have taken as many as 50 fish in one night. That sounds like "enough" to me.

Tackle for swordfish needs to be carefully selected. Not only are these fish fierce fighters, but their soft mouths force fishermen to be conservative in their fighting techniques for fear of a pulled hook. The longer the rod, the farther you can cast live bait, but you don't want it so long that it becomes difficult to keep pressure on a deep fish. I prefer a rod of 6½ feet or slightly less, which I feel is a happy medium. A heavy-action blank is preferred so you can lift the fish, and the aforementioned large guides are needed for casting the bulky wind-on leader. A specialty rod can be ordered from many tackle dealers, and manufacturers such as CalStar and Seeker make weapons specifically designed for sight casting to swordfish.

The Right Reel

I use a reel that I can cast and which holds a minimum of 350 yards of 80-pound line. With the drag set properly, I've had very few swordfish sound and empty the reel. But you need to put the pressure on! This year, I put spectra braided line on my reels and now have over 1,000 yards on the same reels – plus backing – so that the reels are filled to capacity. I also like the idea of minimal stretch. Many anglers don't realize how much of their effort goes into removing the elasticity from monofilament line before they actually put pressure on the fish. Steady, constant pressure is required to beat a swordfish. The more resting you do, the more likely the fish will win.

Star-drag reels with one-piece frames, like the Daiwa Sealine series or Penn Senators with Tiburon or AccuPlate frame conversions, work well for casting. You need the heavier frames to stand up to the amount of pressure required to whip the fish. Star Set, a star-drag handle adapter made by AFTCO, will give you a pre-set drag similar to that of a lever-drag reel. Shimano's graphite lever-drag, two-speed reels are starting to be used by some anglers for casting. The added ability to use the lower gear can really be an advantage when slugging it out with these stubborn brutes.

One of the advantages of trolling for swordfish is that you can use heavy tackle, but keep in mind that you risk pulling the hook if you apply too much pressure. I recommend 80-pound line and a good lever-drag reel, such as the Penn or Shimano 50 or 80 models.

Catching the most prestigious prize in big-game fishing isn't easy, but the level of difficulty makes it an accomplishment of which you can be very proud. Even if you don't target swords specifically, you should be ready whenever you're on the water in case you get the opportunity. It's worth the effort.

Tuna

◆

Bluefin Tuna

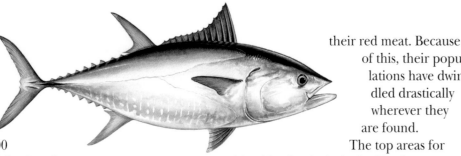

The bluefin tuna is the largest member of the tuna family. The northern species can grow to well over 1,000 pounds; the southern species to over 300 pounds. Bluefin are one of the favorite targets of commercial fishermen due to the high value of their red meat. Because of this, their populations have dwindled drastically wherever they are found.

The top areas for catching bluefins include the Northeastern United States, Newfoundland and North Carolina.

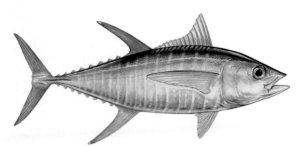

Yellowfin Tuna

A popular sportfish wherever they are found, yellowfin tuna are the most striking in appearance of all of the tuna with vibrant coloration and elongated second dorsal and anal fins. Yellowfin tuna top out at over 350 pounds, but provide a great battle no matter what size they are.

Found in warmer water locations than most other tunas, the top locations for fishing are the Bahamas, Costa Rica, Mexico and New Zealand.

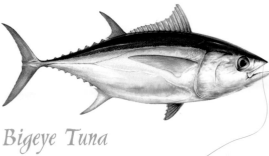

Bigeye Tuna

As their name would suggest, bigeye tuna are recognizable by their oversized eyes and darkly colored back. They can grow to over 400 pounds and are known as one of the strongest fighting tuna species. Like many tuna species, they circle on their way in and challenge an angler's endurance.

The best fishing for bigeye tuna occurs off the coasts of California, Hawaii, the Northeastern United States and Peru.

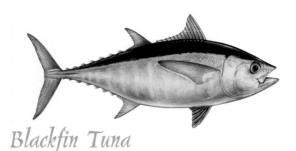

Blackfin Tuna

Most blackfin tuna caught by anglers range from 10 to 25 pounds and are caught on lighter fishing gear. Like the other members of the tuna family they are caught either by trolling lures and bait or by chumming and casting live baits or chunks.

Found in the Atlantic Ocean, blackfin tuna have good populations along the Eastern coast of the United States, Gulf of Mexico and down the coast of South America to Brazil.

Albacore

Found worldwide in warm-water oceans, the albacore is best known for its light-colored meat, which is sold throughout the world as canned tuna. Albacore caught by anglers typically weigh under 25 pounds and are easily recognized by their long pectoral fins that extend beyond the anal fin.

Major commercial fishing operations exist for albacore, but they are also a very popular sportfish. The top fishing areas for albacore include California, Mexico and New Zealand.

YELLOWFIN TUNA

Early-Season Tuna Tactics

by Capt. Mitch Chagnon

In the Northeast, getting early-summer yellowfin and bluefin tuna to eat trolled baits and lures requires some special tricks.

I don't know what's worse: spending all day offshore and catching nothing or spending all day surrounded by tuna that turn up their noses at everything you show them. As many Northeast anglers know, the latter scenario is common in the early part of the season, when schools of yellowfin and bluefin tuna first show up along the 30-fathom line south of Block Island, Rhode Island. However, there are several tactics that often get them to eat when nothing else seems to work.

Beginning in late June and early July, tuna invade the inshore banks of south Cape Cod. Tagging and telemetry studies have shown that tuna use the north-flowing Gulf Stream current as a migration route. When eddies of warm water break off from the Gulf Stream and move inshore, they bring the tuna with them. Cold water off the coast of Cape Cod, brought by influences from the Labrador Current, pushes the tuna in a westerly direction along the banks. The combination of warm Gulf Stream water, rapidly warming inshore waters, and upwellings along the banks creates massive blooms of phytoplankton, the basis of a rich food chain. As the summer progresses, the tuna rest and feed in this warm, bait-filled environment.

Why Won't They Eat?

So why are these fish so hard to catch when they first get here? After discussing the matter with several marine biologists, I discovered the reason.

Tuna have three sources of energy within their bodies. The most readily available source is found in the bloodstream in the form of glucose, or blood sugar. The energy drawn from glucose is responsible for those initial runs that burn out drag washers and spool reels. A second source of energy is stored as glycogen in the liver.

If additional energy is needed, fat stored within the muscle tissues is converted to energy. Animal physiologists compare this last process to the "second wind" experienced by long-distance runners. These fat sources provide tuna with the energy needed for their long migrations.

Since tuna rely on fat reserves while migrating, they feed only periodically and their stomach cavities shrink. The result is that they do not feed as often as tuna that have settled in an area. Because their bodies have been drastically depleted of available energy, they have to be very selective about when and what they eat. They need to receive the maximum energy return for the energy they use to catch their prey. In other words, they will be extremely reluctant to waste energy on anything that might not be food.

Spreader-Bar Solution

To catch fish under these conditions, there are two things you should do: appeal to tuna's competitive instincts, and concentrate on the prime feeding periods of early morning and dusk, when the light is also in your favor.

On my boat, the *Sakarak*, we've found that multiple spreader bars fished close together will work on early-season tuna. We try to be on the grounds by first light so we can fish during the early-morning hours, when the light is low and the tuna can't see the lines, hooks, bars and other terminal gear easily.

Although every boat is different, I've found that a speed of 4.5 to 6 knots is best for trolling spreader bars. Set your outrigger baits as far back as possible, and adjust the line so the closest baits on the spreader bar are barely in the water, with the leader riding out of the water as much as possible. Try to achieve this with all the baits in your spread.

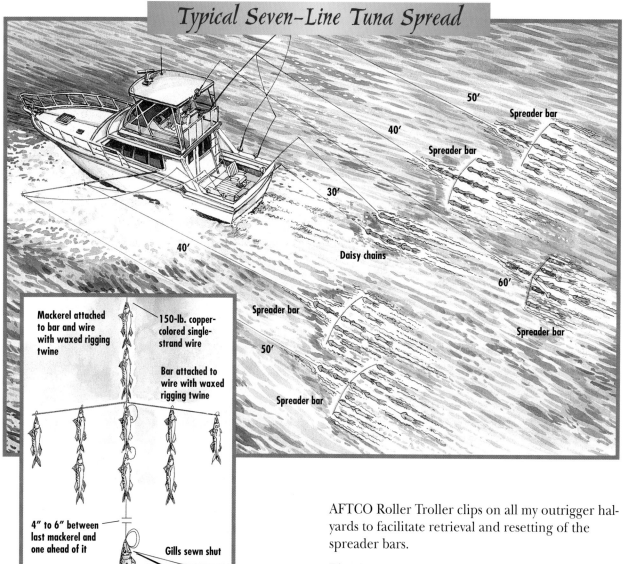

Typical Seven-Line Tuna Spread

50'

Spreader bar

40'

Spreader bar

30'

Daisy chains

60'

Spreader bar

Spreader bar

50'

Spreader bar

40'

Mackerel attached
to bar and wire
with waxed rigging
twine

150-lb. copper-
colored single-
strand wire

Bar attached to
wire with waxed
rigging twine

4" to 6" between
last mackerel and
one ahead of it

Gills sewn shut

Hooked mackerel
larger or smaller
than rest

BRINED-MACKEREL spreader bar.

A Winning Spread

My spread consists of one spreader bar 60 feet
back on the center rigger, two spreader bars off the
long riggers at 50 feet, two more bars off the short
riggers at 40 feet, and two daisy chains on the flat
lines at 30 feet (roughly on the third wave). The
last bait on the main line (the one with the hook
in it) is spaced farther apart than the others on the
bar or chain to make it look weak or injured. I use

AFTCO Roller Troller clips on all my outrigger halyards to facilitate retrieval and resetting of the
spreader bars.

The size of bait I use on my bars depends on the
condition of the seas. On calm days I prefer six-inch
squids rigged on 80-pound coffee-colored wire, and
use the lightest spreader bars available. On rough
days or during low-light conditions I fish larger 12-
inch squids. As for hooks, I use 6/0 Mustad stainless
big-game hooks on the six-inch squids and 9/0s on
the larger squids. Last but not least, I always make
sure the hooks are razor sharp by honing them with
a diamond file on the way to the grounds.

Mackerel can also be used on the spreaders and
daisy chains. I prefer small mackerel; however,
these can be hard to find early in the year, so I
freeze a supply of tinker mackerel when they're
abundant in the fall. I brine them in a cooler of sea
salt and ice immediately after they are caught. I
also add a little formaldehyde to preserve the color
and help toughen the bellies.

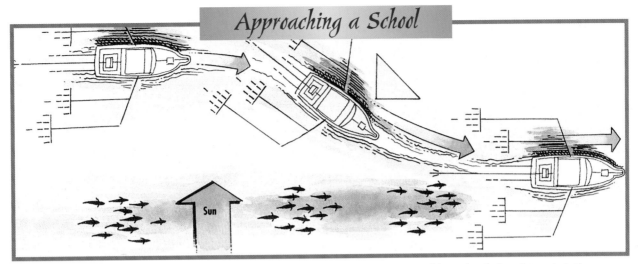

POSITION THE BOAT so its shadow will not pass over the fish. Move ahead of the school by running parallel to it, then slowly angle in so the inside rigger baits swing in front of the lead fish. When all the lines reach the head of the school, straighten out and run in front of the fish, slowing down if necessary to allow them to overtake the baits.

Making Them Strike

Approach and presentation are the real keys to early-season success. Once you locate a school on the surface, approach it at a 40-degree angle, pulling one of the long spreader bars in front of the fish (see diagram above). If the fish make a move toward the baits, leave the rod in its holder and pull the spreader bar away by reeling in the line. If you don't hook up, set the spreader bar back and repeat the process. Sometimes it's necessary to tease the school a couple of times before competition between individual fish gets one to commit to a strike.

On sunny days, always note the position of the sun and your angle of approach, since the shadow of your boat falling over the school could put the fish down. If conditions prevent an angled approach, get far ahead of the school, slow down, and wait for the fish to come to you. Then make a turn to either side to position one of the long rigger bars in front of the school. Once the fish turn to investigate, use the teasing technique and pull the baits away from them.

Many times the fish will follow a particular bait and suddenly hit one of the others. Multiple strikes are common, especially with schools of 40- to 50-pound fish. If you get a fish to follow a bait, watch the other lines carefully. If possible, have a crewman on every rod, ready to pull the offering away from the fish as soon as he sees a follow.

The Jig Trick

Even after tuna have settled down in their summer feeding grounds, they can still be fussy, leisurely cruising around and pushing bait. You'll often see this on bluebird days, when bright sun and calm waters give tuna the edge. Their keen vision can detect the faintest irregularity in your baits and turn them off immediately, creating unbelievable frustration for the fisherman.

But while lots of fish are visible on the surface, there are more underneath where the light is reduced. Those are the fish I target. Capt. Dick Lema clued me in on a technique for dealing with fussy tuna on bright days. He learned it from Montauk captain Carl Darenberg, who was known for producing fish in tough conditions.

Lema chooses a jig that matches the size of the bait the fish are chasing. He casts it into the school and allows it to sink 50 or 60 feet, where there is less light. The lure is then retrieved as quickly as possible with a quick jigging action. This imitates a wounded baitfish struggling to return to its school – an easy meal for tuna!

The first days of the offshore season and the first schools of tuna will get anyone's adrenaline pumping, but try to stay cool and take your time. If you see someone working a school, give them room, and if you hook up, leave the school and let the next guy have a shot at them. Proper etiquette and a little patience and courtesy will not only make your day more enjoyable, you won't be as likely to spook the fish.

Cast to a Tuna

by George Poveromo

Tuna on casting gear? Off Venice, Louisiana, the local charter crews make it look easy.

If you think fishing for 100-pound yellowfin tuna on 12-pound test is crazy, how about doing it from an anchored boat? The light-tackle part we had planned, but we hadn't counted on the missing anchor float.

While Capt. Mike Frenette rigged a 50-pound-class stand-up outfit, still hot after discovering his float ball was missing, I cast a small MirrOlure to one of the big yellowfins swimming back and forth in the chum slick. Maybe it was tempting fate, but I couldn't resist. Unlike the smaller tunas we'd been catching earlier, this one ignored the lure. Instead, it fed selectively on the bonito chunks we had been tossing over.

I asked Frenette's assistant, Darrin Perches, to throw a heaping helping of bonito chunks into the slick once a yellowfin reappeared. He did, and I cast my lure right into the morsels, leaving the reel in free-spool. The fish almost fell for the lure, which drifted back with the chunks, but turned away at the last moment. On the next try, however, it mistook the piece of plastic for a fleshy tidbit and engulfed it.

You can imagine how quickly a 100-pound yellowfin can dispose of 12-pound line. There was no sense in thumbing the spool (I made sure mine wasn't anywhere near it!), so I just held on. As the line neared the arbor of my reel, I tightened the drag and braced myself. The fish stopped momentarily, then charged off, obliterating what faint hope I had of turning it toward the boat. Fortunately for the fish, the line parted close to the leader.

Hot Spot for Yellowfins

I was fishing with Frenette and Perches on the tuna grounds off Venice, Louisiana (below). Situated some 21 miles up the Mississippi River from South Pass, this modest town exists because of commercial fishing and petroleum interests. The Venice Marina, which sits directly across from a fish-processing house and marina for long-liners, shrimpers and other commercial vessels, is the only facility catering to sportsmen who seek access to the open Gulf, and it's a hopping place on those bluebird weekends.

VENICE, LOUISIANA and surrounding area.

Because of the nutrients pouring into the ocean from the Mississippi, plus the profusion of oil platforms that serve as mini-ecosystems, these waters offer some of the best and most diverse fishing in the U.S. Offshore. It's yellowfin tuna that keep the Venice Marina's boat launching facilities full and the local charter captains busy.

There are two major runs of yellowfins during the year off Venice. We were fishing the late-winter/spring run, which is primarily made up of tuna between 30 and 60 pounds. These fish normally show between February and May, and thin out to occasional catches by summer. The big run for fish over 100 pounds occurs between August and November. Even though the 100- to 150-pound fish are most plentiful during the fall run, they're fairly common during the spring as well. What's more, both seasons offer fantastic blackfin tuna fishing, especially for fish in the 30-pound class.

Casting to Tuna

On this trip, we planned to draw the fish behind the transom with chum, then cast lures to them. I brought a cooler of frozen block chum with me from Florida, while Frenette rounded up several cases of mullet and menhaden.

With the chum and gear all set to go, we sped down the Mississippi in the *Teaser H* – Frenette's twin-powered Pro-Line 27 – through Tiger Pass, and into the open Gulf, en route to the Midnight Lump. This muddy hump, which rises from a depth of 420 feet to about 212 feet, is a hot area for tuna.

Once we arrived, we determined how the current and light wind would affect our position, then dropped anchor on top of the mound. I put a frozen chum block into a mesh bag and tied it to the transom. As the particles and oil from the melting chum seeped toward the drop-off, Frenette began dicing bait and throwing chunks of it into the forming slick.

Between the calm sea and the polarizing effect of the slick, visibility was good. Before long, a pair of

TUNA CHUM ready for action.

yellowfins appeared. These early arrivals were highly aggressive, and fought desperately over the fish scraps. I broke out a 12-pound-class outfit and cast a MirrOlure into the slick. Sensing the competition between the two yellowfins, I began twitching the lure in place, its shiny sides reflecting sunlight through the water. One of the fish charged the lure, sucked it in, and spat it out instantly. I cast again. This time I saw the fish swim up slowly behind the lure, inhale it, and turn away. I set the hook and settled in for a long fight, which ended when Frenette slipped a gaff into the 47-pound tuna.

Catching tuna on lures and casting gear is exciting, but it can become very frustrating when the fish start feeding selectively. They'll still fall for a lure, but you have to do some fine-tuning to fool them.

The Importance of Chum

Tuna first respond to the scent of the frozen chum and are then drawn behind the transom by the chunks of bait. Oily baitfish such as menhaden and bonito (the fresher the better) usually work best for the chunks.

As long as handfuls of diced meat are dispersed regularly, the tuna should stay in the chum slick. The trick is to use enough chunks to hold their interest, not fill them up. However, with the number of tuna off Venice, you'll probably run out of chum long before you fill their stomachs.

The lures you use should closely match the size and shape of the chunks you're throwing into the slick, since the tuna become programmed to feed on them. On our venture, we used MirrOlure 43 MR 21s, Rapala SL13s, Mr. Wiffle grubs, Acme spoons and Blue Fox spoons.

Because of the water clarity and tuna's sensitivity to terminal gear, we rigged with monofilament leaders no heavier than 50-pound test, with some as light as 15-pound. In case a wahoo or kingfish decided to show up, we had an outfit with a wire leader at the ready. When the current dropped off and the bait chunks sank slowly, sinking lures performed best. Because the tuna would dart from the perimeter to

ambush the chunks, we kept the lures sinking among the fish particles; the swimming plugs, spoons, and Mr. Wiffle grubs were carefully worked during the descent so they would wobble and flash. As long as the lures stayed with the chum, they'd fool the tuna. Once the chum was eaten, or had disappeared in the depths, the lure was retrieved and the process repeated.

Dealing with Current

The best feeding blitzes occurred when the current was running hard, but this created the problem of keeping the lure near the surface among the drifting chunks. To stay in the action, we used surface plugs and rigged the plastic grubs on bare hooks.

At one point, the chunks were simultaneously assaulted by a mix of yellowfin, blackfin and even kingfish. However, if the lure we were using wasn't imitating a piece of bait, it was rarely noticed by any of the species. One of the best lures was a four-inch, clear-with-silver-glitter Mr. Wiffle grub, which closely resembled the chunks.

The small, deep-diving Rapalas and sinking MirrOlures also proved successful, but were fished in a different way. Instead of floating them back with the chum, we cast them out about 40 feet and then placed the rods in the holders. Fish would hit the lures as they fluttered and flashed in the current.

Another trick for keeping a lure in the strike zone is to stick a small Styrofoam packing "peanut" or piece of surgical tubing over one of the treble hooks to keep it floating at the same level as the chum. You can fine-tune the depth by changing the amount of material added to the lure. A small piece of sponge is also excellent for slowing a plug's descent. By experimenting with the size of the sponge particle and the gradual weight it acquires by absorbing water, you'll be able to precisely match the chum's sink rate.

Over a two-day tuna blitz, we boated yellowfins pushing 60 pounds and blackfins to 32 pounds. If you're serious about tangling with tunas on light tackle, consider Venice. Some days it's as easy as shooting fish in a barrel!

TUNA:

Banking on Bluefins

by Angelo Cuanang

Your primer for cashing in on the fall run of bluefin tuna off the coast of central California.

Within 20 minutes of passing the color change, we knew we had arrived at the right spot. Clouds of feeding shearwaters darkened the rolling waves, but what really got our blood boiling was the sight of big, blue torpedoes crashing the surface.

Turning the boat in a wide arc, we pulled our jigs along the perimeter of the school. Seconds later, one rod doubled over, immediately followed by another, and another. Triple hookup! My brother Abe and buddy Rich Shears quickly grabbed the outside rods while I took the middle.

But it was soon clear that we were in trouble. The 4/0 reels we were using suddenly looked like tiny baitcasters. Even though they were loaded to the rim with 40-pound line, and their drags were locked down, it wasn't enough. We were going to get dumped if we didn't do something – and fast!

It was far too rough to back down, so I turned the bow upsea in the direction of the fleeing fish no easy matter in the four- to six-footers rolling our way. Waves crashed over the bow, yet we were able to gain some line. Just when it seemed like the move might pay off, all three lines became tangled.

As expected, two lines burned off, leaving me to slug it out with the remaining fish. Rich took the helm and jockeyed the boat, keeping the line to the windward side. An hour later, he and Abe planted two gaffs in the fish, and the three of us heaved aboard a beautiful 130-pound bluefin.

Action by the Bay

This adrenaline-pumping encounter didn't take place off Baja, Costa Rica or some other famous blue-water locale. Amazingly enough, it occurred just 32 miles southwest of San Francisco. And best of all, it was no fluke. Bluefins, like albacore, range up and down the western coast of California. Granted, they don't always appear in significant numbers, but when conditions are right they can be found feeding right alongside the albies.

Our bluefins aren't the giants found on the East Coast. Most of the fish landed off central California range from 40 to 180 pounds. Bigger fish estimated at over 200 pounds have been hooked, but not landed, largely due to inadequate tackle. Off Santa Cruz, the major hot spot in previous years, anglers were hooking bluefins on albacore tackle, which led to some epic battles lasting three to five hours.

During "normal," non-El Niño years, cold-water upwellings of nutrients along the deep-water banks and canyon edges create a rich soup of plankton for baitfish to dine on. And that may be why both albacore and bluefins have appeared relatively close to shore over the last few seasons.

Albacore are normally the main offshore target for local anglers in the late summer and early fall. The average season runs from late July to early October. The bluefins seem to show up a little later than the albies, with late August, September and October being prime time.

Autumn Hot Spots

In the early fall, bluefins often begin to appear on some of the traditional albacore grounds, such as the Monterey Canyon, outside Santa Cruz at the weather buoy, the 601 and the Guide Seamount.

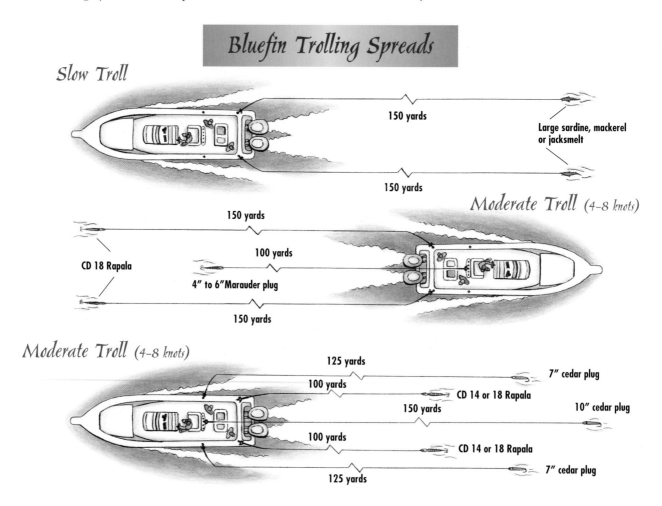

Bluefin Trolling Spreads

Slow Troll

150 yards

Large sardine, mackerel or jacksmelt

150 yards

Moderate Troll (4–8 knots)

150 yards

100 yards

CD 18 Rapala

4" to 6" Marauder plug

150 yards

Moderate Troll (4–8 knots)

125 yards — 7" cedar plug

100 yards — CD 14 or 18 Rapala

150 yards — 10" cedar plug

100 yards — CD 14 or 18 Rapala

125 yards — 7" cedar plug

Continuing up the line, the Pioneer Seamount, Pioneer Canyon, the Dumping Site and the area west of the Farallons can also produce.

Bluefins have a special affinity for deep-water contours or edges, especially if bait is present, which is why passing schools sometimes appear on the western edge of Fanny Shoals. Heading north to Bodega, the edge of the shelf off the Cordell Banks can yield action, as well. These northern locations don't always produce, especially during cold-water years. A call to a local tackle shop is the best way to find out if the big boys are there or not.

Bluefins are powerful fish, allowing no margin for error when it comes to tackle. Rig up with a 6/0, a 50, or a 50W reel loaded with 50- to 80-pound monofilament. Match the reel to a 5½- to six-foot stand-up rod rated for the line you're using.

Make sure you have a quality fighting belt and a shoulder or kidney harness that's set up for stand-up fishing.

Top Tuna Tempters

Trolling jigs from six to eight knots can be productive, but bluefins tend to be shy of boats, so place the jigs well behind the boat, especially in calm water. To minimize problems, I'll often troll just three lines.

Productive trolling jigs include Zukers in Mexican flag and zucchini patterns, zucchini Sevenstrand Tuna Clones, and green-and-white hexheads. Cedar plugs, diving plugs such as Rapala countdowns and small Marauder plugs can draw strikes. Bluefins can be leader-shy, so rig your jigs with a three-foot section of 80-pound fluorocarbon and a 7/0 double hook. If the fish are very shy, tie the jigs directly to the main line.

To locate the action, watch for bird activity or breaking fish. You will often see large concentrations of shearwaters, terns or seagulls pounding the surface in areas where tuna are chasing bait. Bluefins tend to feed in tighter packs than albacore, and often move quickly in a straight line. This makes it fairly

easy for anglers to locate the leading edge of the school.

Should you locate a feeding school, don't run through it. Determine the fish's direction of travel and make a long, wide arc in front of them. This will minimize boat contact with the school, while at the same time presenting the lures in front of the fish. If this approach doesn't work, live bait may be your best bet.

Live-Bait Tactics

Live mackerel is the top choice, but mackerel can be hard to come by. In this case, large sardines and even jacksmelt can be used. When using sardines, rig the bait by pinning it crosswise through its nostrils with a 5/0 to 8/0 live-bait hook or, even better, an Owner Mutu circle hook. Use an extremely long dropback of 100 to 200 yards and slow-troll the bait in front of the school.

When slow-trolling live bait, keep the rod tip up and the reel in free-spool while maintaining thumb tension. If you get a pick up, point the rod at the fish, free-spool line for three to five seconds, then lock up and hang on.

To beat a bluefin you must apply relentless pressure throughout the battle. Try "short stroking" to keep the fish's head coming toward the boat. Short stroking involves making brief lifts of the rod to pull the fish up, then quickly recovering line on the downstroke. When you feel the fish coming to the surface, pour on the pressure.

Always keep the line directly in front of you throughout the battle. This is especially important if two or more fish are hooked at the same time, as it minimizes the risk of a tangle. Equally important, the skipper must maneuver the boat to keep the angler in the best fighting position. The line should always angle away from the boat, ideally on the windward side. This prevents the angler from being pinned to the rail, and minimizes the chance of the line being cut on the side of the boat or engine prop. It's clearly a game a teamwork, but if everyone does his job, a big bluefin will make the ride home with you.

TUNA:

The Joy of Giants

by Al Ristori

Catching and releasing 10 or 20 giant bluefin tuna a day is no big deal over the wrecks off Hatteras, North Carolina.

Would you believe a fishery in which anglers who have spent years and thousands of dollars trying to catch their first giant tuna hook up in a matter of seconds? Or giants that hit frozen bunkers as readily as a school of ravenous bluefish? If you don't believe it, then you obviously haven't heard about what's been happening off Cape Hatteras, North Carolina.

After just two days of fishing the wrecks south of Hatteras in March, everything I thought I knew about giant tuna after a quarter century of fishing for them went right into the circular file. Not only were medium and giant bluefins available in huge quantities, but they usually fed with such abandon that it was impossible to equate them with the same picky fish that drive most anglers to distraction.

The weather was so marginal when Capt. Paul Spencer headed south from Hatteras with his 57-foot *Sizzler* on March 4 that we were the only sportfishing boat working the *Proteus*, a wreck in 20 fathoms lying about 24 miles and 190 degrees from the inlet.

An Eerie Scene

In the course of an hour, we passed through an incredible range of water temperatures, starting with 47 degrees in the harbor, to 50 degrees in the inlet, and a 10-degree jump from 58 to 68 degrees at about 20 miles. At this point it seemed as if we were entering a different world. The northeast wind,

which had been only about 15 mph back on shore, escalated to 25 mph, and seas increased from two to six feet. The water temperature jumped even further to 72 degrees by the time we reached the wreck, and the interaction between the tropical water and the 45-degree air temperature produced patches of steam that rose from the surface and occasionally masked the three gillnet boats that were working the area.

Joining me on this adventure were Marsha and Len Bierman, who had been aboard the *Sizzler* during the last weekend in January in an attempt to add the release of a giant tuna to Marsha's many stand-up fishing accomplishments. However, that turned out to be the only period last winter when the bluefins abandoned the wrecks, due to an influx of cooler water. Lee O'Brian, a powerful young Australian deckhand and rugby player who was visiting the Biermans, was also aboard on this trip, along with Penn Fishing

Tackle President and veteran angler, Herb Henze.

At first, Spencer didn't mark anything on his fishfinder except bluefish and became worried about a repeat of the previous trip. However, huge boils appeared behind the boat soon after mate Charles Perry started throwing frozen bunkers over the side. A bunker attached to 28 feet of 300-pound Momoi leader was tossed in, and Marsha was instantly hooked up to a giant. That fish was fought on

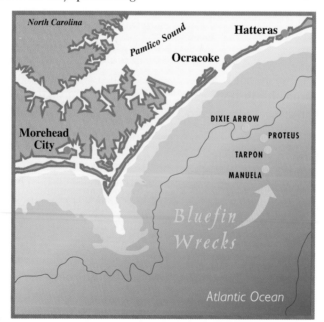

A 734-POUND Bluefin Tuna.

50-pound stand-up tackle for 37 minutes before the hook pulled, but Marsha later released a medium in the 250-pound class on the same gear in 50 minutes.

It was too rough for stand-up fishing, so Marsha decided to wait for better conditions. Fighting from the chair for the first time since 1986, she whipped bluefins ranging from 250 to 500 pounds in about 10 minutes each, as did the rest of us, except for Len, who was recovering from a shoulder operation.

Bluefin Surface Blitz

The 12th tuna was being fought around 2:00 when the ocean suddenly came alive with bluefins jumping clear of the water. At first we thought they were chasing bluefish, but it soon became obvious that they were after small fish about six inches long. Spencer thought they might be cigar minnows. Shortly thereafter we spotted a school of bluefish chasing the same bait. Since the chunking bite had suddenly stopped when the unusual surface activity began, Perry caught a blue and trolled it live – the technique used for these giants the previous two winters.

Having no success with the bluefish, Perry tried trolling a ballyhoo and soon Henze had another bluefin to the boat for release. The last shot went to O'Brian, and he hooked something on the ballyhoo that didn't put much of a bend in the 130-pound gear. It turned out to be a huge blackfin in the 30- to 40-pound class.

The next day turned out to be a repeat of the first, except for the addition of seven other boats from Hatteras and Morehead City. The seas were even larger and the fog thicker, so the stand-up tackle was put aside again in favor of fighting from the chair. Marsha released nine, and could have caught many more if she hadn't stepped aside so that O'Brian and I could flex our muscles on seven more.

The competition among the boats didn't seem to make a bit of difference in the morning, since hookups occurred almost immediately after Perry started tossing bunkers overboard. However, there was an early-afternoon period when the fish got picky, and Perry decided to drop down to a 200-pound leader. That did the job right away, but before the 10-minute fight was over, Bob Eakes reported from the *Bullfrog* that the tuna had turned on again. Sure enough, it was back to instant hookups with 300-pound leaders, and we left them biting better than ever.

Giants ... on Poppers!

As spectacular as our fishing seemed, it was actually somewhat below par compared to what occurred over the next couple of weeks, especially during the relatively calm weekdays. Even before we got there, Spencer had recorded only one day (except for the Biermans' weekend) with fewer than 10 releases since January, and on that day his elderly charter client decided to return early after having released four giants in 12-foot seas. Many days saw tuna boiling all around the boat, and they were so hot at times that anglers were getting strikes by casting hookless poppers!

Catches of 10 to 30 fish a day were routine in March, and many scores higher than that were posted. Eakes, who owns Red Drum Tackle in Buxton, took friends out on his 35-foot custom-built *Bullfrog* several times a week from February 1 into mid-April and released about 450 bluefins, of which roughly 350 were tagged. His best day produced 54 releases.

Eakes said one of his releases was in the 1,000-pound class, although he saw a 1,200-pounder in the slick. Four more fish were estimated to be in the 900-pound class, 20 were said to be around 800 pounds, and 100 were estimated at 500 pounds or more.

Fast Fights Save Fish

Regardless of size, it appears that these fish can be caught in 15 minutes or less on standard giant-tuna tackle. In fact, the majority of fish are released within 5 to 10 minutes. The relatively shallow water prevents the tuna from sounding, and they seem inclined to remain near the wreck after being hooked. Even Marsha's light-tackle tuna never took much line and were fought within 100 yards of the wreck. The other major factor behind the shorter fighting times is the use of long leaders, which result in the mate's doing a large portion of the hardest work when the fish is near the boat.

Short fights are probably the best thing for the tuna. Brad Chase, a Massachusetts scientist who has been studying release mortality, endorses the practice. He took blood samples of fish in January and March, and has noted a correlation between fighting time and stress indicators found in the blood.

Another important factor in fish survival appears to be the use of circle hooks. Eakes said that after changing to circle hooks (he uses both the Mustad 16/0 circle hook and the VMC #3) he missed very few strikes, virtually stopped pulling hooks, and never had a gut-hooked fish. He said every tuna is hooked in the corner of the jaw, and he feels that any hooks left in a fish will fall out over a period of time. Eakes told how he had caught a tuna he had tagged exactly one month earlier, and the hook was gone.

While there has to be some mortality among the released fish, The National Marine Fisheries Service (NMFS) hasn't been able to quantify it in any way. Rumors that NMFS divers found 35 tuna lying on the bottom are unfounded. What they did find around the wreck, however, were dead bluefish, which may have been the result of fallout from gill-netting operations.

How Big Are They?

The vast numbers of bluefins caught day after day from the *Proteus* and four other nearby wrecks in depths of 90 to 125 feet are strange enough, but the variation in sizes is even more puzzling. Eakes said it often seems as if different schools have moved in overnight. Indeed, many of the bluefins we caught on the first day were large mediums, and one fish probably didn't even go 150 pounds. Yet the next day only a couple were mediums, while the rest were small giants up to 500 or 550 pounds.

The actual size of these fish is open to debate, because most of the local skippers release their tuna. I felt that our crew was being fairly conservative in their estimates. On our trip, Spencer told me he hadn't seen any fish up to that point which looked to be over 600 pounds, and said the average size was around 350 pounds. Perry, who fishes all over the world with top anglers such as Stewart Campbell, agreed with those estimates.

Capt. Bob Pisano, the godfather of New Jersey giant-tuna fishing and a man who has tangled with hundreds of giants over the years, fished aboard the *Candlewick Lady* out of Hatteras toward the end of March. He said that 14 of the boat's 17 tuna were in the 250-pound class, with two being 350-pounders and one around 500 pounds. Many anglers who fished there in March were able to keep an angling-category small medium of under 70 inches, tuna in the 150- to 220-pound class.

Healthy Fish

Sebastian Bell of the New England Aquarium has been inspecting Hatteras tuna specimens provided by NMFS. He has been selecting for the largest possible fish, but couldn't come up with anything that weighed over 400 pounds, and says that the size estimates given by anglers have been "a bit optimistic." Bell also stated that the fish he's studied so far have been very healthy, and contain a high fat content. However, their stomachs have contained only chum and a few bluefish bones.

It was originally assumed that bluefish, which have wintered around the wrecks for decades, were attracting the tuna, but there's little evidence to support that theory. It doesn't seem to make sense that the bluefish would stick around if hounded by tuna, or that tuna could exist on such relatively difficult prey to capture.

If there's any natural bait holding the tuna in the area, it's not obvious. Yet the fish are in very good condition. The chunking itself may be a big factor in attracting and holding the tuna, just as happened a few years ago at the *Bacardi* wreck off New York and New Jersey.

Another mystery is why none of the tuna inspected were ripe with roe. Winter is the spawning time for bluefins, and any fish over 350 pounds should be mature. Still, Bell found no indication of spawning activity.

Migration Mystery

Where these tuna come from and where they go is also unknown. Although they look and fight like the bluefins we know up north, the Hatteras tuna are so eager to eat that it's hard to believe they could be the same fish. Not only do the Hatteras fish gobble up floating frozen bunkers, Perry once even hooked one on a chicken wing!

The NMFS expects to start getting answers to the migration question, since over 1,000 bluefins were tagged. It anticipates no changes in the regulation of the winter fishery, but urges anglers to use circle hooks and heavy tackle to keep mortality low. As of now, it will remain a release fishery, since the season for large mediums and giants doesn't open until June 1. The only exceptions will be for those boats possessing an incidental catch permit that allows one tuna to be kept per year providing the fish is not sold. Anglers seeking light-tackle records should check for charter boats that still have an unused permit, since there's a good possibility the fish may be killed.

Will the giants be back on the wrecks next winter? That's anyone's guess, because even Carolinians can't agree as to how long they've been there. Some say they were spotted years ago and no one bothered with them. Others claim the giants have been in the area only recently, and that recent winters were a phenomenon that will not be repeated.

In any case, if you want the surest shot you'll ever, have of catching a giant tuna, there's no better bet than to fish the wrecks off Hatteras or Morehead City from January to early April. Capt. Walter Spruill of the *Hatteras Fever* was shut out during the first weekend in April for the first time in 22 trips, and the fishery appeared to be over. However, a party boat found the tuna there again the next week, and Eakes had a 30-fish day on April 11. It then died down to a couple per day during Easter week, and was all over by the following week.

It's best to schedule a trip for a weekday in order to avoid a mob scene, which usually turns the fish off after a few hours. And be prepared to wait it out ashore during some windy days. It never seems to be rough enough to turn the tuna off, but catch results have been much better in good weather. However, those without cast-iron stomachs and plenty of experience in giant-tuna fishing are better off accepting the skipper's word when he deems it too nasty to fish.

Canyons, Cont....

by Al Ristori

If you're a die-hard offshore nut who bemoans the approach of winter, don't stow your gear just yet! The season just got a little longer.

Younger readers may not know it, but until a few decades ago albacore, yellowfin and bigeye tuna were rarely caught in the waters off New York and New Jersey. Then some adventurous souls started running 80 miles offshore, where they discovered another world influenced by Gulf Stream eddies and populated by semi-tropical species. These fish are now the backbone of the Mid-Atlantic offshore fisheries – and not just for a few short summer months, as was, until very recently, the case.

Would you believe that hot yellowfin action could be enjoyed off New York and New Jersey in November and December, when most anglers are concerning themselves with striped bass or planning winter vacations to Florida and the Caribbean? Having gone that far, what would you say if you heard that tuna were being brought back to the New Jersey docks in January?

Well, it happened in 2000, and for the first time there was a real winter canyon fishery out of New Jersey.

Indeed, the action didn't end until a few anglers had scored the first tuna of the new millennium.

What's going on out there? Was that year a freak, or is this something we can count on? Should anglers from Virginia to New England cancel their winter long-range trips out of San Diego now that they can tangle with tuna 100 miles from home?

The answers remain largely speculative, but it appears that the fish have always been there. Longliners have been catching winter tuna in the canyons for decades, long after most anglers called it quits. Len Belcaro of Offshore Services, a provider of satellite ocean-temperature charts, remembers years when warm water prevailed well into fall. However, until he stopped sending out charts after mid-October due to lack of interest.

What is clear is that the calendar is not very significant when it comes to the movements of pelagic fish in the canyons. Much more important are eddies of warm, blue water that spin off from the Gulf Stream and swing toward shore. Regardless of the time of year, there's a good chance of catching semi-tropical fish whenever such eddies move within range of the offshore fleet. For example, Captain Paul Dalick Jr. on the *Moondancer* out of the Brielle Yacht Club caught a yellowfin and several school bluefin up to 50 pounds as early as May 29, 1999, when an eddy moved into Baltimore Canyon. Even more noteworthy, Captain Dave Matthews of the Manasquan boat *Pepper* released the 1999 season's first blue marlin, a 400-pounder, in Hudson Canyon in mid-June.

Blue Water Moves In

Infusions of blue, warm water bring exotic species far inshore many summers, but last year was most unusual. In August, blue water moved in so close that it almost touched the beaches off northern New Jersey, and frigate mackerel (the smallest member of the tuna clan) were often seen chasing baitfish in the surf. On August 9, I was hosting Kevin Noonan of Lake Elsinor, California, when he caught a 10-pound skipjack tuna in 30 feet of water off Monmouth Beach, within sight of the New York City skyscrapers.

Yellowfin tuna moved into areas only 20 miles or so off northern New Jersey, and were even closer off Montauk. The numbers weren't huge, but the fact

that even one or two were caught per day was remarkable. It was definitely shaping up to be a weird summer. Indeed, I got a second shock on August 18 when Noonan released a 27-inch bluefin tuna caught at Manasquan Ridge. It was unusual enough for a bluefin to be hooked at a 50-foot lump only six miles from Manasquan Inlet, but Kevin's father, Bob, got an even bigger surprise when he took the next hit. As this larger tuna was brought alongside, Joe Blaze looked down and identified it as a yellowfin of about 35 pounds! We then added a skipjack to complete a New Jersey nearshore tuna slam that will be hard to match.

Even blue marlin and wahoo were encountered inshore during that period, along with dolphin, which are regular summer visitors to the Mud Hole. At least five blues were hooked by trollers seeking tuna within 25 miles, and Captain Gary Williams released a 300-pounder from the *Lucky 29*. When the blue water broke up after a storm, practically all of the exotics left, even though the water temperature remained over 70 degrees.

While water temperature certainly plays an important role offshore, water color and bait availability appear to have a greater influence over the presence of game fish in deeper water. For example, while inshore yellowfins usually depart when the temperature drops below 70 degrees, canyon yellowfins will remain in water that's ten degrees colder as long as the bait sticks around. By the end of that year it appeared that the trick to catching yellowfins in quantity was to follow the last of the 60-degree water as it slowly moved south.

Ironically, in the very year that the National Marine Fisheries Service (NMFS) imposed a "proactive" three-yellowfin limit on recreational fishermen, the species was the most abundant it had been in at least a decade – especially fish in the 30- to 60-pound class. Night chunking for yellowfins normally turns on sometime after the middle of August, with Labor Day being a safe time to start scheduling overnighters for consistently good action. Storms fouled up the fishing in early September, but yellowfin limits became routine that month, except on nice weekends when the sheer volume of boats dictated that not every one would be able to hold fish.

Finding a window of good weather is the key to an almost sure thing in Hudson Canyon during the fall, and last season saw some great fishing. Charter boats that sailed by late morning or early afternoon for overnighters often limited out within a couple of hours and were heading back before midnight. Even party boats regularly caught limits of yellowfins, along with some albacore and an occasional swordfish or mako.

Yellowfins gradually switch from a night bite in August and September to a daytime bite as water temperatures drop in the fall. While this was generally the case last year, night bites remained frequent into December. In another departure from the norm, there were times when jigs out-produced bait in the dark last fall.

Yellowfin fishing was even hotter by the end of October, and anglers on the party boat *Jamaica* from Brielle, New Jersey, were limiting out on many trips. Water temperatures dropped to the low 60s in November, but the fishing didn't miss a beat. The temperature actually climbed back up to 65 degrees on November 18 before falling again shortly thereafter.

The Bite Goes On

Fishing the northern canyons usually ends for most charter boats by mid- to late October, primarily because of the threat of bad weather. Party boats often continue their trips into November, though few plan on sailing beyond mid-month. As in years past, most skippers packed it in when the yellowfin bite was still hot last November, while a few kept adding trips to take advantage of the fishing.

The *Jamaica* was one of the few party boats that hung in there, and its trips kept stretching farther into the fall. Captain Howard Bogan Jr. reported that his customers tallied over 90 tuna from 30 to 60 pounds on the December 12 trip, but the fish were nowhere to be found on December 19. On that day the water temperature had dropped to 60.5 degrees and a northeaster was blowing 20 to 25 knots. Only a few albacore were boated at night, and there was no action in the previously hot area by 9:00 A.M., so Bogan moved two miles to the west. Here the temperature rose one degree, and the *Jamaica* got into three hours of action with much larger yellowfins. Fifteen fish from 70 to 130 pounds were boated, and several others were broken off.

With the satellite showing warmer water moving south, Bogan made his last trip of the year on December 27, a 105-mile run to Wilmington Canyon where Gulf Stream eddies were still providing the desired 60.3-degree water temperature. While fishing there wasn't up to previous standards, the latest-ever New Jersey offshore tuna catch got started just before first light as nine yellowfin were hooked from 4:45 A.M. to 5:15 A.M. (only three were boated). Two more were caught during the next hour, but the best bite occurred when the tuna began schooling 100 to 180 feet below the Jamaica at 6:45. After that there was a steady pick on both bait and jigs, with the action continuing for the rest of the morning to provide a total catch of 25 yellowfins from 30 to 50 pounds, plus seven albacore from 45 to 60 pounds.

In order to boat the first tuna of the new century, Bogan scheduled a trip for January 3, but it turned out he was too late. Beating him to the punch was Ken Avon, who sailed from Manasquan Inlet to the Wilmington on New Year's afternoon and lucked out with a flat-calm, mild night. His temperature gauge died on the way south, but Gary Caputi of Offshore Services was aboard and the two took a shot at stopping where the last 60.3-degree water had appeared on the satellite image two days earlier. Caputi said it felt warm there, and they ended up fishing in shirtsleeves the next morning. Though there were lots of squid under the lights, nothing hit at night. But, there was a blast of 55- to 60-pound albacore at first light, and Avon boated the first of the new millennium.

The *Jamaica* ran to the Wilmington the next evening and managed two 30-pound yellowfins, allowing the anglers aboard to claim bragging rights to the first Jersey yellowfins of the century.

It's anyone's guess as to whether we'll enjoy another endless canyon season like the last. Some years the blue water disappears and water temperatures drop quickly, forcing northern charter and party boat skippers to sail to southern canyons to finish up their scheduled trips. Yet, as this was being written in early March, satellite images were still showing 58- to 60-degree waters as far north as the Hudson.

There's no forecasting what effect storms will have in the fall or how far the Gulf Stream eddies will travel, but anything is possible. So keep an eye on the blue water, pick a window of good weather, and don't get caught short by missing some of the year's best sport long after the crowds are gone.

Tracking Tuna through Science

by Rob Goodwin

Greg Skomal, a biologist for the Massachusetts Division of Marine Fisheries (MDMF), is working to address some of the questions surrounding the survivorship of released fish. Skomal's research, supported by the federal Sportfish Restoration Fund, uses acoustic tracking technology and blood sampling to determine the effects of capture on sharks, tuna and marlin.

"Our primary goal is to assess post-capture survivorship and behavior; our secondary goal is to observe behavior in New England waters," Skomal said. He and other MDMF biologists have developed a system for measuring the stress caused by angling capture and correlating these measurements to mortality. First, the fish is fought for a predetermined amount of time or until exhaustion. Next, a blood sample is taken from the fish from which blood gases and other indicators of physical stress can be measured. Last, the fish is released with either a traditional tag or an acoustic transmitter. The transmitter allows Skomal to track the fish with a directional hydrophone and assess its post-stress behavior and survivorship.

In the 1999 season, Skomal and his crew added a yellowfin and a young bluefin to their list of successful tracks. On August 4, Skomal and his crew caught a yellowfin south of Nantucket and fitted it with an acoustic tag to monitor its survival and behavior. The fish didn't lead its followers miles away, but remained in the general area, seemingly undergoing a brief recovery from capture. The fish then spent the rest of the day swimming between 60- and 90-foot depths along a nine-degree thermocline. Skomal hypothesizes that the fish avoided the hot, 76-degree surface, instead favoring the cool, 60-degree water near the thermocline and foraging on the bait that congregated there.

On August 25, Skomal responded to reports of small bluefin in the shallow rips several miles off Nantucket — an occurrence that had never before been recorded. The biologist found small bluefin feeding on squid and baitfish, so he captured one, released it and tracked it, observing its behavior in an unusual environment. Like the yellowfin, the small bluefin survived and headed offshore, back into more predictable habitat. Skomal speculates that ideal water temperatures and an abundance of bait lured the fish inshore, but it is difficult to explain the activity, by tracking a single fish.

The tuna tracked in 1999 add to years of encouraging results. Since 1993, Skomal and his associates have sampled 12 species and tracked over 300 tuna, sharks and marlin to examine the effects of catch-and-release. His research has shown that angling causes the fish significant stress, but released fish do survive if handled properly. Skomal asserts that "fish can recover if correctly handled and with a minimum of trauma." He adds that "efforts should be made to resuscitate tuna and marlin after exhaustive bouts longer than 15 minutes."

Skomal suggests leaving the hook in the mouth of sharks and tuna and using the leader to drag them through the water, as many anglers don't try to resuscitate them because they have no bill to grab. Of the many fish released and tracked by Skomal and his team since 1993, only one didn't survive, a giant bluefin that was released east of Cape Cod without being resuscitated.

A GIANT bluefin tuna about to be tagged.

Other Offshore Species

DOLPHIN

Wahoo

Reaching weights in excess of 100 pounds, this member of the mackerel family is sometimes disdained when it shows up and wreaks havoc in lure spreads deployed for billfish.

Most of the time however, the wahoo is a welcome sight to fishermen who target them for their jarring strikes, blazing runs and firm white meat.

In addition, the fact that wahoo are a schooling fish often leads to sudden fast action and multiple strikes. Wahoo prefer shiny or brightly colored lures.

King Mackerel (Kingfish)

A close relative of the wahoo, the king mackerel or "kingfish" is a prized sportfish throughout the Atlantic Ocean and Gulf of Mexico. They are often the target of tournament fishermen, who enjoy the challenge of trying to locate and catch kingfish, which can grow to 90 pounds.

Kingfish are a migratory, pelagic species that are most often found in schools of fish weighing from 8 to 20 pounds.

Dolphin

Often seen as a "trip saver" for charter boat captains that are having a tough time catching their target species, the often easy-to-catch common dolphin is found in good numbers in tropical waters throughout the world.

These beautiful fish are often referred to as dorado or mahimahi and can grow to 80 pounds. They are excellent table fare and are often found under objects floating on the open ocean.

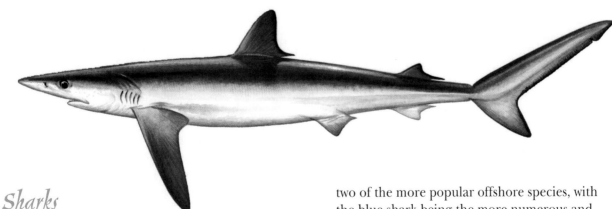

Sharks

Regionally popular, sharks are becoming a target species, in part because of declining populations of other offshore species such as the swordfish in the Northeastern United States, for example.

The blue shark (above) and mako shark are two of the more popular offshore species, with the blue shark being the more numerous and widely distributed. They reach sizes of over 400 pounds. The mako shark is known for its great fighting ability, which can include spectacular jumps and its exposed teeth (p. 80) that give it a fearsome appearance.

Wahoo on a Wire

by George Poveromo

Want to increase your catch of wahoo?
Try high–speed trolling with wire line.

Few captains know how to wire-line for wahoo better than Capt. Ron Schatman. Known as "Dr. Wire Line" throughout the Bahamas, Schatman has used wire to bag everything from king mackerel to sharks during a colorful 33-year charter career that has taken him from New Jersey to Miami.

Today, Schatman is a hot commodity as a freelance captain, particularly throughout the Bahamas, where he worked the cockpit during the capture of a 920-pound blue marlin – the third largest in the country's history – and pioneered deep dropping/electric-reel fishing for huge wreck fish and a host of deepwater snappers. His forte, however, is wire-line fishing for wahoo.

Tools of the Trade

When it comes to wire-lining wahoo, there are arguably few people in Schatman's league, and he has either won or placed in the money at more tournaments than his competitors care to remember. The list includes a win in the November 1995 Bacardi Rum wahoo tournament in Bimini, where his team bagged 18 fish in three days, including a 57-pounder. He once produced 28 wahoo in a day and as many as 23 fish in a three-hour period. His heaviest fish to date is a 90-pounder taken in the Bahamas. His wire-line rigging and trolling techniques might seem unorthodox to some, but they've played a big part in these catches and continue to be instrumental in his success.

For wire-line fishing, Schatman prefers an 80-pound-class rod with either hardened rollers or tungsten-carbide ring guides, and a swivel tip. He opts for a curved butt over a straight one because most of his fish are fought straight from the gunwale rod holders. Also, curved butts keep the lines closer to and more parallel with the water, reducing the chances of a kink.

Schatman fishes two-speed Duel reels in 6/0 and 9/0 sizes, as well as two-speed Penn Intentional 50s. He prefers the two-speeds because the low gearing gives him the flexibility to check bait or shake off weeds without slowing down, as well as the cranking power to keep a big fish coming his way. He uses the higher gearing to keep a tight line on a fish that's running with the boat, or to keep one skipping across the surface should it rise on plane. However, he points out that the venerable 9/0 Penn Senator, a popular workhorse model, is much more economical.

Many anglers prefer Monel, a softer and more expensive alternative to stainless wire. According to Schatman, Monel might be softer and a little easier to use, but it's not worth the expense. "With Monel, you're practically forced to use Dacron or monofilament backing," he says. "That's because it's roughly twice as expensive as stainless wire. Monel costs 20-plus dollars a pound, whereas I can buy a quality grade of stainless for about $10 to $12 a pound. It takes about five pounds of stainless to fill a 9/0 reel, and I rarely use any backing on a 9/0.

"I fill my reels entirely with American Wire 316L, .028 (80-pound-test) stainless wire. The 316 designation is the grade of stainless, whereas the .028 is its diameter. It's a quality, low-carbon wire that doesn't rust or break prematurely from pitting like the old 304-grade stainless wire we used to fish with. In fact, minor bends can be straightened by hand."

Keeping stainless wire in tip-top shape however requires a thorough fresh water rinsing after each use. If the outfit is going to be racked for a while, pull out some line after the washing process and dry it by reeling it back through a towel. A light misting with spray lubricant is also recommended.

Schatman trolls between 12 and 15 knots, claiming slower speeds aren't effective. "Sure, you can bag a wahoo or two going slower, but you really run the numbers up when you're pulling fast. When they see those lures ripping by, it drives them nuts. We're not talking about catching a fish here and there; we're talking triple- and even quadruple-headers when we pull across a pod fish. You should see the faces on the people aboard the other boats when I go barreling by them at a 15-knot trolling speed. They think I'm crazy ... until they see the fish we catch!

"Under most conditions, my standard trolling weight is 16 ounces, but I often use two-pounders. The heavier weights are recommended in seas over four to five feet to keep the baits down. But remember, I troll a lot faster than most anglers, so I'll upgrade to a two-pound weight whenever my baits begin to break the surface. Overall, though, I try to fish as light as possible if I can get away with it. On average, figuring 80-pound gear, a two-pound weight and 15-knot trolling speed, a bait that's about 100 feet back should ride within two feet of the surface."

The Real Reason for Wire

"Contrary to popular belief, you're not really seeking lure depth when using wire. In fact, it's irrelevant. For wahoo, you want the baits racing just below the surface. Wire line is preferred because it slices through the water at the speeds we're going. It has a quick entry, trolls very uniformly, and it really drives the hooks home because there's no stretch and hardly any belly. I also mix in a monofilament outfit or two in my spread, but the wire lines are much more durable. Monofilament outfits are a little more sporting, but the line accumulates nicks and abrasions. Monofilament just doesn't seem to hold up to the stress that is created by the combination of heavy weights, high speeds and a lot of fish. It always seems like we're cutting back the line and re-rigging the monofilament, but you can fish wire day after day without worrying about re-spooling. However, the reason I mix in a monofilament outfit or two is because their baits will ride a little higher than those on the wire, even with the same amount of weight. That helps us fish four subsurface lines without the threat of a tangle during a tight turn."

Schatman fishes four outfits, straight from the gunwales. The flat-line reels closest to the transom are each filled with 80-pound monofilament and the lines are rigged with two-pound weights. One is positioned roughly on the first wave and the other about 200 feet back – the farthest bait in the spread. The short wire line rig is positioned between 75 and 100 feet back, while the long wire line is set about 150 feet back. They're fished from the angled rod holders, behind the flat lines.

"The other key to this operation is the bait," says Schatman. "I use a heavy, bullet-headed, straight-running lure in front of a dual-hook horse ballyhoo. The bait must have some weight at those speeds too. Plus, if a wahoo cuts off the bait and doesn't get hooked, the lure's still there to draw another strike. There's always something flashing and dancing on the hooks.

Hot Wahoo Rigs

"I use lures between four and six ounces, more specifically, the R&S Tuna Dart, the Mini Dart, and the C&H Wahoo Whacker. Color doesn't make a difference. In fact, I start with a variety of shades. Black, pink, purple, red, orange – it just doesn't make a difference. They whack them all. Very rarely will you see one color hog the action. If that happens, try fishing more of that particular color.

"For the type of setup explained here, I use a six-foot leader made of either No. 10 stainless leader wire or No. 9 piano wire, both of which test at about 130 pounds. Keep in mind that stainless leader wire is not the stuff you spool on your reel, since it's much stiffer and won't last long. A good leader for this style of fishing is stainless wire between No. 10 and 15, or piano wire between No. 9 and 12.

"The difference between piano wire and stainless wire is primarily the price. Piano wire averages between $8 and $12 a pound, while a pound of stainless leader wire costs between $24 and $30. Piano wire is more expendable and will rust within a couple of days. I don't save my leaders. I make them up, fish them, and throw them out. Piano wire also lays out straighter than stainless leader wire.

"I rig my lures with two double-strength 10/0 hooks. The lead hook, a No. 3412C Mustad, is a needle-eye version, while the trailing hook is a round-eye Mustad No. 3407SS. To connect the two, open the eye of the trailing hook, place it around the shank of the lead hook, and press it closed. It doesn't make a difference whether the hooks are in line with each other or at 180-degree angles."

Watch for Surprise Strikes

Schatman recommends engaging the reel clicker while dropping back to set the spread and keeping your thumb on the side of the spool to maintain pressure. Keep the other hand near the drag lever in case of a strike. Don't put your fingers on the wire, which could pinch some flesh or sever a finger if it backlashes on a surprise strike.

After the lures are positioned, Schatman advances the strike drag, which is set at approximately 15 pounds. On the strike, Schatman prefers to keep the boat moving, and only slows down well after the fish has been hooked. "Keeping the boat moving at trolling speed often results in multiple hook-ups," says Schatman. "Don't be in a great rush to slow down after hooking up. When you start to bring the fish in, keep the wire coming in smoothly and steadily. If anything, use short pumps, not long ones that could kink the wire. When the weight comes up it's the angler's responsibility to reel it right to the rod tip and prevent it from swinging around. Once we decide whether to keep the fish or release it, we replace the damaged bait and get it back into the water, ASAP. With a good crew you can do this in a matter of seconds. And don't forget to watch the other baits while all this is going on; wahoo hit them on the fall, and again when the boat picks up speed."

Hunting for 'Hoos

When searching for wahoo in the Bahamas, especially off Bimini, Schatman looks for clean blue water, bait, a steep drop-off, or a color change. If the current's running hard and blue water is tight to the drop-off, fishing is bound to be good. Under these conditions he'll troll between 150 and 600 feet of water. When there's little current, the incoming tide could be an ally by pushing blue water against the drop. An outgoing tide can dirty the water and produce poor fishing, unless a strong current holds the blue water/dirty water edge inshore of the drop or somewhere along the fishing zone, establishing a sharp color change.

Schatman also uses his wire-line techniques off South Florida, where he's caught as many as seven wahoo in a day. Off South Florida, he fishes the clean side of color changes, as well as any rips, weedlines, and floating debris he finds between 250 and 400 feet of water. When a wahoo is hooked, the

GPS coordinates are stored so the area can be fished thoroughly.

Schatman's advice for those considering a wire-line outfit, is to avoid buying a reel that's too small for the task. "For wahoo, you don't want anything smaller than a 9/0. Wahoo will run off a lot of line, and a big one will dump a 4/0 and perhaps a 6/0. You also need the line capacity in case you kink the wire and have to re-rig. Stick with 80-pound-class wire, which is very durable. The lighter you go, the more you'll have to change the wire. And don't get lazy and leave the outfit at home just because it might be big and bulky. Fish it regularly and you'll see that wahoo aren't as uncommon as you may have thought."

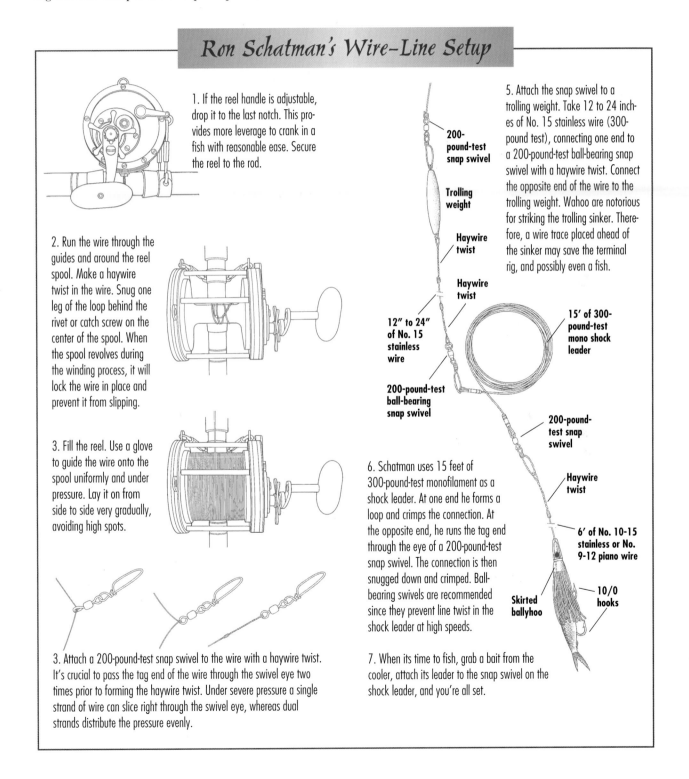

Ron Schatman's Wire–Line Setup

1. If the reel handle is adjustable, drop it to the last notch. This provides more leverage to crank in a fish with reasonable ease. Secure the reel to the rod.

2. Run the wire through the guides and around the reel spool. Make a haywire twist in the wire. Snug one leg of the loop behind the rivet or catch screw on the center of the spool. When the spool revolves during the winding process, it will lock the wire in place and prevent it from slipping.

3. Fill the reel. Use a glove to guide the wire onto the spool uniformly and under pressure. Lay it on from side to side very gradually, avoiding high spots.

3. Attach a 200-pound-test snap swivel to the wire with a haywire twist. It's crucial to pass the tag end of the wire through the swivel eye two times prior to forming the haywire twist. Under severe pressure a single strand of wire can slice right through the swivel eye, whereas dual strands distribute the pressure evenly.

200-pound-test snap swivel

Trolling weight

Haywire twist

Haywire twist

12" to 24" of No. 15 stainless wire

200-pound-test ball-bearing snap swivel

5. Attach the snap swivel to a trolling weight. Take 12 to 24 inches of No. 15 stainless wire (300-pound test), connecting one end to a 200-pound-test ball-bearing snap swivel with a haywire twist. Connect the opposite end of the wire to the trolling weight. Wahoo are notorious for striking the trolling sinker. Therefore, a wire trace placed ahead of the sinker may save the terminal rig, and possibly even a fish.

15' of 300-pound-test mono shock leader

200-pound-test snap swivel

Haywire twist

6' of No. 10-15 stainless or No. 9-12 piano wire

10/0 hooks

Skirted ballyhoo

6. Schatman uses 15 feet of 300-pound-test monofilament as a shock leader. At one end he forms a loop and crimps the connection. At the opposite end, he runs the tag end through the eye of a 200-pound-test snap swivel. The connection is then snugged down and crimped. Ball-bearing swivels are recommended since they prevent line twist in the shock leader at high speeds.

7. When its time to fish, grab a bait from the cooler, attach its leader to the snap swivel on the shock leader, and you're all set.

Baja's Bomb Squad

by Chuck Garrison

If you're a long-range angler or want to increase your wahoo action, make sure you have an assortment of these deadly wahoo lures in your arsenal.

When Eric Dahlkamp took his first long-range trip aboard a San Diego-based sportfisher last year, cruising deep into Baja waters, he bombed in a big way. So big, in fact, that the 26-year-old returned to port with one of the largest wahoo ever pulled from Mexican waters. His huge 'hoo weighed 124.5 pounds and is believed to be the second largest ever taken on a San Diego long-range boat, surpassed only by a 129-pounder caught in the late '70s. The reason Dahlkamp "bombed" is because of the lure he was using, a creation that has proven absolutely deadly on wahoo.

"Bomb" is the generic term coined by long-range fishermen to describe a type of casting lure – either manufactured commercially or homemade – that basically consists of a heavy, chrome-over-lead jig head wrapped with a vinyl skirt. A wire leader is threaded through the center of the head and terminates in a large, single hook.

Why It Works

Wahoo love bombs, so much so that they have become the casting lures of choice for most wahoo anglers. Since its inception in the early 1980s, the bomb has evolved into several variations, with adornments ranging from shiny tinsel to flashy tape to bright spinner blades.

The bomb was born when long-range fishermen started experimenting with casting lures that would hook and, more importantly, hold more wahoo. Back then, plenty of strikes came on the popular, cast-metal irons or jigs like the Salas, Tady, UFO and Sea Strike. Still, too many fish got away. Replacing the lure's treble hooks with long-shank single hooks helped put more fish on deck, but a major problem persisted: since the heavy lure remained next to the fish's mouth, the wahoo could easily dislodge the hook by shaking its head.

"What was needed was a lure that would slide up the line once a wahoo was hooked," recalls Carl Newell, an avid long-range angler from Glendale, California, and the manufacturer of the high-speed, graphite reels that bear his name. "That way the wahoo couldn't use the weight of the lure to shake the hook loose."

So Newell, an engineering type, began tinkering and came up with a casting lure that was similar to a small trolling lure. It had a heavy, bullet-shaped, chrome head adorned with a soft-vinyl skirt. Partially hidden beneath the skirt was a single 8/0 to 10/0 hook. Newell called his creation the Caster. Fishermen soon realized the effectiveness of Newell's design. Some even started making their own and began calling them "bombs."

Besides Newell's Casters, other commercially made bombs include versions by Doc "Ski" and Braid Products, all available in area tackle shops. Many anglers, however, prefer to make their own versions.

Bomb Takes a Monster

It was just such a homemade bomb that Dahlkamp used to hook his monster wahoo while fishing some floating kelp paddies near the Toussaint Bank, located about 625 miles south of San Diego. While catching several wahoo in two days of great fishing on the "kelps," Dahlkamp had lost all of the bombs he had assembled before the trip. As a last resort he built a makeshift model using a slip-sinker, tinsel, wire leader, a steel Mason ring and a VMC 8/0 hook. One angler aboard described Dahlkamp's crude creation as "a pellet with fins."

As the boat slid up to yet another clump of kelp, Dahlkamp fired off his red-and-silver bomb and immediately got a strike – the only hookup that came from that spot. Less than 20 minutes later he had the six-foot fish on deck.

Richard Hightower of La Mirada, California, is another bomb builder who's always experimenting. On one of his ten-day trips aboard the *Qualifier 105*, Hightower tested his idea of using a modified hook angle to increase his percentage of landed wahoo.

"I think a lot of my success on that trip had to do with offsetting and bending the hook," Hightower explains. "I offset the 8/0, long-shank Siwash hook, which changed the angle of penetration, and I also slightly bent in the end of the hook itself. I think that really helped the hook stay in the fish."

Did it ever. On Hightower's first day of fishing he batted a thousand, hooking seven wahoo, and landing every one of them. By the end of the trip he had caught 18 wahoo, and even had to hand off several of the fish to other anglers.

Hightower offset his hooks at home. Using a vise to hold the pointed end of the hook, he applied pressure to the shank to create about an eight- to ten-degree offset. He used a pair of Vise Grips to slightly bend in the hook point.

Bow Launch Station

While fishing, Hightower chose to stay away from several fishermen who were using live-bait rigs and bunching up in the stem. Instead, he cast from the bow, a technique that works well when bombing for wahoo. His strategy is to cast out at a 45-degree angle from the bow as the boat slides to a stop next to a kelp paddy or following a trolling hookup. Hightower lets the bomb sink to a depth of 40 or 50 feet, then puts his high-speed reel in gear and starts cranking.

"After a while, guys started to notice that every time we had a good stop I'd be coming down the rail again with another hookup," Hightower chuckled. "Pretty soon most of the guys on board were throwing bombs, too."

Bomb-Fishing Tips

We asked Newell, Hightower, Rothery, Captain John Klein (the new owner and operator of the *Qualifier 105*) and other veteran long-range pros some questions about bomb-fishing techniques. Here are their answers:

• Use on dark mornings or on overcast days. Two-color combinations of black, dark red, deep purple, and orange have been consistent wahoo-catching colors.

• The first bombs to hit the water are often the first – or only – ones to be struck. Stand ready at the rail and cast out as soon as the boat stops.

• After casting, be alert for a strike as the bomb is sinking. If the line suddenly jumps and races, you've been struck. Immediately put the reel in gear and wind rapidly until the line comes tight, then keep winding. Don't stop winding to set the hook, and don't raise the rod tip. Keep the rod pointing in the same direction as the line and don't raise the tip until the fish begins taking line against the drag.

• Use the same technique when a wahoo hits the bomb on the retrieve. Let the wahoo turn and run against a moderately tight drag, hooking itself in the process.

• When fighting a wahoo, minimize the traditional "pumping" of the rod. Keep the line absolutely tight. When you must pump the rod to retrieve line, use short lifts.

• A high-speed reel (5:1 or 6:1) is recommended. The faster reel moves the bomb at a swift pace, which excites the wahoo and also makes a day of casting less fatiguing. High-speed reels also take up line faster and minimize slack when a wahoo runs toward the boat.

• Keep your hooks super sharp. At times, a wahoo's steel-like mouth may seem impenetrable – and it will be if you're using dull hooks. Carry a small file or battery-operated hook honer in your tackle box for on-the-spot touch-ups.

How to Build a Bomb

1. Thread a length of 77- or 88-pound-test, dark, single-strand wire leader through the chrome head. The finished leader should be about 28 to 30 inches long.

2. Use a No. 7 black, steel ring to connect the end of the leader to the hook eye. Attach the ring to the wire via a haywire twist.

3. Slip the ring on an open-eyed Mustad 95103XS hook before crimping the hook eye closed.

4. Attach the vinyl or Mylar skirt material around the molded shoulder of the head by wrapping with a strip of quarter-inch reflective prism tape.

5. Optional flash can be added by attaching a spinner blade to the hook. Slide a 1/0 barrel swivel over the point of the hook and onto the shank; then use a No. 2 or No. 3 split ring to attach the swivel to the spinner blade. A popular blade style is a No. 4 or No. 5 Colorado spinner blade in a hammered-silver finish.

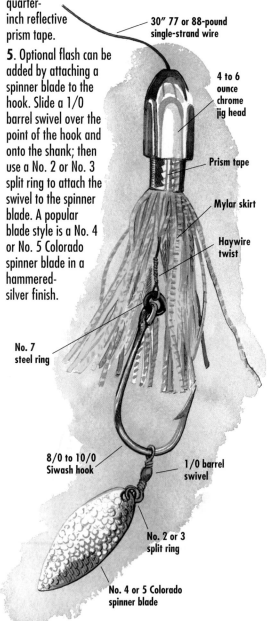

30" 77 or 88-pound single-strand wire

4 to 6 ounce chrome jig head

Prism tape

Mylar skirt

Haywire twist

No. 7 steel ring

8/0 to 10/0 Siwash hook

1/0 barrel swivel

No. 2 or 3 split ring

No. 4 or 5 Colorado spinner blade

Five on Kings

by John E. Phillips

*Five tournament pros reveal their strategies for
finding and taking the biggest king mackerel.*

When it comes to hard-core fishing, the members of the Southern Kingfish Association take the term to a new level. These guys and gals regularly take a beating as they roar far offshore at speeds of up to 60 miles per hour in pursuit of big kings.

To the casual observer, the thought of hurtling through three- to six-foot seas for hours on end might seem insane, as if something more than teeth had been knocked loose in the process. However, there's a method to the madness, one that could mean big fish and big bucks for those willing to make such long, uncomfortable runs.

"Big kings usually hold in 80 to 185 feet of water," explains Terry Waldrop of Gulfport, Mississippi, captain of the *Isle of Capri* tournament boat. "But that doesn't mean you can run to just any wreck, reef or rig and expect to score."

I fished with Waldrop on a practice day before the Isle of Capri King Master 100, an invitational tournament held at the Isle of Capri Casino in Biloxi. Like most kingfish tournament competitors, Waldrop's boat is a fast one, and we fairly flew over the wavetops as we sped 75 miles offshore to troll around some deep-water oil and gas rigs.

"The rigs hold a tremendous amount of baitfish," Waldrop points out. "You'll usually find the kings where you find the bait. However, since not every rig holds good-sized kings, we hit as many as we can until we locate the big ones."

When Waldrop arrives at a rig, he baits up with dead ribbonfish that he buys from the Killer Bee Bait Company and sends them down on his downriggers. He fishes the ribbonfish on 25-pound "camo" main line and rigs them with a 1/0 single hook in the head and four Bystrong No. 4 treble hooks along the body. The middle three trebles are simply strung on the wire leader, which makes it very easy to rig the long baitfish. So far he's never had the sliding hooks kink the wire.

Waldrop always fishes one or two ribbonfish among the live blue runners in his four- or five-line spread, even though they draw more strikes from the medium to small kings. "The ribbonfish simply let me know if the kings are in the area," Waldrop explains, "but most of the really big fish will attack the blue runners."

Waldrop cuts the fins off his ribbonfish to keep them from spinning, since the kings won't hit a bait that spins. When he's searching the area, he'll fish the ribbonfish on his downriggers, with the deepest bait placed halfway to the bottom. Once he locates the kings, he may replace one of the ribbonfish with a live blue runner to target bigger fish.

Love Those Livies!

Live bait is the key to catching big kings for another pro – 1998 SKA national champion Forest Taylor of Ocean Isle Beach, North Carolina. "You are most likely to catch really big king mackerel if you get the best live bait available," states Taylor, who prefers to fish with live menhaden, cigar minnows or ribbonfish. He tries to catch his bait near the structure he plans to fish, using a castnet or a bait-catcher Sabiki rig. Instead of trolling for kings, Taylor prefers to fish directly over underwater structure, and employs the use of chum.

"I run a 1/0 hook through the bait's nose, with a 6/0 stinger hook attached to three or four inches of wire placed in the back of the bait. I like to fish 20-pound main line; however, if the fish are acting shy I'll scale down to 15-pound."

Speed Pays

To win a kingfish tournament, the first thing you have to do is pinpoint the location of the biggest kings during the practice days. However, sometimes several fishermen will discover the same schools in the same locations. That's where a fast boat comes in handy.

Steve Shook and his wife Ginger of Golden Meadow, Louisiana, won the titles of SKA Top Man and Woman Angler of the Year in 1998, along with four boats and a quarter million dollars in cash. They agree that a fast boat gives them an edge. "We fish from a 35-foot

Donzi rigged with three 250-hp engines," Steve says. "With this power, we can do 70 mph, which can get us to a spot faster than most of the competition."

The Shooks also gain an edge by experimenting with new products and techniques. "Currently, I'm testing titanium leader material," Steve reveals. "This wire won't kink or break, and I haven't lost a fish with it yet. It offers a definite advantage, and I believe it will become the new leader material of serious king mackerel fishermen." Steve also fishes with tiny, experimental titanium hooks, and uses line as light as ten- or 12-pound test, especially if the water is really clear and the mackerel aren't biting on heavier line. Unfortunately, the general public will have to wait a little longer to get its hands on the new titanium leaders and hooks, since the products are still being refined by the manufacturer.

Steve and Ginger use their boat for more than simply getting to and from the fishing grounds in record time. It also plays a valuable role in their fish-fighting strategy. "We chase the fish with the boat when the mackerel makes its usual two runs," Steve explains. "This way I don't put too much pressure on the line. A large king will normally make a 100-yard run after you first hook it, followed by a 200-yard run. After that the fish generally sounds.

"Once it goes deep, we'll back off the drag and motor upwind or upcurrent of its position. Then we'll try to reel the fish to the surface, letting it swim toward us instead of away from us. The fish generally surfaces beside the boat, which allows us to quickly and easily gaff it and bring it onboard."

Patience Pays

Joel Wood of Murrells Inlet, South Carolina, has fished for king mackerel for 11 years, winning several local and national tournaments. He believes that patience will reward you with a trophy king.

"If I see plenty of bait on my depthsounder, as well as gulls diving for the bait, I'll stay on a spot longer than most fishermen will," Wood says. "King mackerel will come to where the baitfish are. Just because you can't catch them right away doesn't mean they aren't there." It could be that they've just eaten and aren't hungry.

"If I find a spot with plenty of baitfish and birds, I know the kings will show up eventually. If I start catching fish, I'll stay on the spot for at least three hours, trying to catch a big one. If not, I'll usually leave after an hour and a half of intense fishing. However, if the baitfish remain in that spot I may stick with the area a little longer. Most anglers leave after going 45 minutes without a bite. Often, after they leave, I'll catch a nice king."

Chum Bombs & Purple Squid

Ed Mecchella of St. Simons Island, Georgia, the 41st person to join the SKA as a charter member, has fished in nearly every tournament the association has held, winning six of them. "I believe that really big kings lead solitary lives," Mecchella says. "They prefer to stay alone in open water."

Mecchella believes that rigs and wrecks, while serving as baitfish magnets, often hold smaller kings. However, he says that schools of bait in open water are where you'll find the real smokers.

"If I locate a large school of baitfish in open water I'll mark the spot with my GPS. Then I'll try to hold my boat over the school and sink one or two bags of frozen chum all the way to the bottom. As the chum thaws, it floats to the surface, bringing the baitfish, and the kings, with it. When that happens I can catch the kings by trolling ribbonfish and blue runners over the site where I've dropped the chum. If I take a nice king, I may drop another bag of frozen chum to keep the baitfish and kings actively feeding in that area."

Over the years, Mecchella has experimented with lots of different baits and rigs, including some pretty unusual ones. "The strangest bait I've ever caught a king mackerel on was an eight-inch, purple squid marketed by Killer Bee Baits," Mecchella recalls. "We rigged the squid like we would a ribbonfish, placing a 1/0 hook on the end of the wire leader and three treble hooks on a section of wire attached to the shank of the first hook. I was surprised when a king took that big squid; over the years I've learned that versatility with your bait and tackle will often produce the biggest fish."

Similar to many other top anglers, Mecchella likes to fish with 12-pound line, which results in more strikes and, ultimately, more kings. "On line that light, I'll use 27-pound wire leader," Mecchella says. "Most anglers fish with a heavier leader, but I believe that lighter wire doesn't spook the kings as easily and gives my bait more action."

Are you sensing a pattern? While each of the pros interviewed for this article does things slightly differently, certain similarities apply. One is the belief in live bait as the key to catching big kings; another is the use of light line and terminal tackle to fool wary fish. But perhaps the real common denominator is the desire to put in long hours and run great distances in punishing conditions to find that one tournament-winning fish. It's what hard-core fishing is all about.

Five-Line Slow-Troll Spread

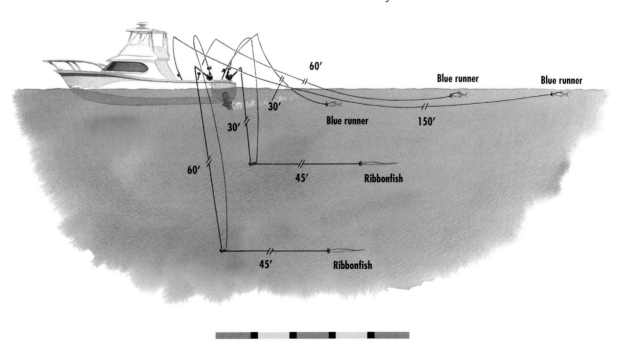

60'

Blue runner   Blue runner

30'

Blue runner   150'

30'

60'

45'   Ribbonfish

45'   Ribbonfish

More Kings Faster!

by John E. Phillips

Now that king mackerel are becoming more numerous along the Gulf Coast, savvy skippers and anglers are figuring out ways to fill their limits quicker while targeting bigger fish at the same time.

How much should I tip a millionaire?" the man asked the mate at the conclusion of a half-day charter aboard the *Desperado*. The first mate smiled. "Whatever you think I'm worth."

All morning he had baited lines, gaffed fish and helped the man and his family catch their limit of king mackerel. This deckhand has fished all his life, but he also has a second job. When he's not on the road playing lead guitar for the country band Alabama or in the studio cutting albums, Jeff Cook is out in the Gulf chasing king mackerel, a species that he's seen grow in number and size over the last few years. Today a party of six can usually take a limit of two kings per person in a half-day of trolling. Just three or four years ago that would have taken all day!

From May to October, kings can be found cruising just a few hundred yards off the beach, so there's no need to make long runs to secret hot spots or own a lot of expensive navigation equipment. Many anglers credit the Florida net ban, along with the reduced size and catch limits, for the incredible kingfish comeback.

Hal Aiken, Cook's long-time fishing partner and captain of the *Desperado*, has fished out of Destin, Florida, for more than ten years. He offers another reason for the improved fishing. "I believe more king mackerel are being caught nowadays because people have changed the way they fish for them," he says. "In the past we pulled feather dusters and spoons on heavy tackle to catch kings, but now we've discovered that light line and live bait produce more fish."

Rigging for Success

When Aiken and Cook troll for kings they use 12- to 20-pound monofilament. Because the lighter line is less visible, it results in more strikes and, ultimately, more fish in the boat. It's also more fun for their customers to use, since the lighter drag results in a longer and more dramatic fight.

For live-bait fishing, the pair tie on a barrel swivel and attach 2½ to three feet of No. 4 or No. 5 single-strand, coffee-colored wire leader, which is less visible than braided wire. On the end of the wire Aiken twists on a No. 4 treble hook. "Because Jeff and I use live bait that's sometimes hard to come by, we fish with treble hooks instead of singles," explains Aiken. "You'll get plenty of strikes with single hooks, but you won't catch nearly as many fish."

Aiken and Cook use a two-hook setup on their bait rigs by attaching a second treble to the eye of the first with a four- to six-inch piece of the single-strand wire. This second hook makes it less likely that a king will cut the bait in half without getting hooked. "When you troll live bait without a second hook, you reduce your bait coverage by half, and you'll miss more fish than you'll catch," Aiken points out.

Aiken places the first hook in the nose of the bait so it will track straight behind the boat, but leaves the second hook swinging freely alongside the bait's body. "I don't attach the second hook because the bait can't move naturally with two hooks in it," Aiken explains. "I also feel that a second hook makes it hard for the bait to stay upright and swim straight behind the boat."

Although the net ban has helped increase the number of king mackerel in the Gulf, it has also made bait more difficult to obtain. Instead of buying it from local netters, charter captains must now catch their own. "We prefer cigar minnows because king mackerel naturally feed on them in our area," says Aiken, "but we'll also use herring. Basically, we catch whatever bait we find close to the beach before moving offshore in search of kings."

Slow-Troll for Success

Aiken's bait spread consists of two flat lines fished from the center of the stem and two lines fished off the down riggers. To find the fish he simply trolls parallel to the shoreline while looking for activity on his depthsounder. "The depth of the water determines the depth of my downrigger baits," says Aiken. "For instance, if I'm in 80 feet of water I'll set my downriggers at 30 to 35 feet. If I don't get a strike at that depth I'll set the baits deeper, perhaps at 60 feet."

Aiken points out that a king hooked in deep water will often draw the rest of the school to the surface as it's being brought in. That's where the flat lines come in.

Once the kings start biting near the surface he turns the boat in tight circles to stay on top of the school.

One of Aiken's tricks for big kings is to troll very slowly. "I center my rudder and keep the boat moving forward by simply putting one engine in gear, which allows me to troll at about three knots. I know I take bigger kings by trolling slower."

Aiken and Cook generally set their flat lines 60 to 70 feet behind the boat. However, in a stiff wind they shorten that distance to about 30 feet to keep the lines from tangling during a turn. According to Aiken, the boat doesn't seem to bother the fish as long as they're up and feeding. "If you hit an active school of kings, they'll often take your baits as soon as you drop them in the water," he says.

As mentioned, the use of light dictates a light drag and steady pressure on the angler's part. Ideally, the drag should allow a big fish to make between two and four runs. However, too light a drag may give the fish time to work the hook loose.

Usually, the fish will hook itself on the strike, so there's no need to yank back hard on the rod. Aiken's wife June, who also serves as a deckhand on the *Desperado*, often coaches the anglers after a hookup. "I tell them to let the fish take line – don't try to stop it," she says. "The more line in the water, the more it will slow the fish down. Just give the rod three or four quick jerks to make sure the hook is set firmly."

Lots of Smokers

For proof that Aiken's methods account for huge kings, one need only look at his logbook. Last season his charter customers boated 35 kings over 35 pounds, including eight that weighed 40 to 45 pounds. "The average weight of the king mackerel caught off Destin is five to eight pounds. However, when you use live bait the size increases to between 10 and 12 pounds," says Aiken.

"The net ban and the two-fish, 20-inch (fork length) limit are allowing fishermen to catch more and bigger kings than ever before. The large number of fish we've seen and the increase in size proves that the fishing off Destin has drastically improved."

If you plan to visit the Gulf and want to fish all day, I suggest devoting a half day to king mackerel and then spending the rest of your time targeting snapper, grouper, triggerfish or amberjack. With so many kings in the Gulf today, variety fishing is wide open.

Run and Gun for Dolphin

by George Poveromo

An exciting way of targeting one of South Florida's favorite summer game fish.

The race began as the sun peeked above the horizon, shedding enough light to guide us across the calm sea. I accelerated hard, forcing the crew to grab their hats and the T-top rail as we headed for the Gulf Stream off Palm Beach, Florida.

A half-hour later we spotted a large patch of weeds on the horizon. I steered toward it and pushed the throttles to the console. After reaching the weed-line, which spanned more than a mile, I shut down while my partner began fan-casting a jig along the edge. I backed him up by chumming the handfuls of cut bait. We'd fish a section of the weedline for about five minutes, then cruise ahead a couple hundred feet and repeat the process.

The first four attempts failed to produce a strike and we began to think about leaving. Just then, several seagulls began hovering above the weeds about 100 yards downcurrent. At first we thought they were excited over the bait chunks, but when they began shrieking and darting toward the water, I had a hunch we were about to score big.

We stayed where we were and coaxed the activity closer by tossing diced Spanish sardines into the water. As I had suspected, the birds were shadowing a huge school of dolphin that came right to the boat.

For the next hour, we had a blast fighting these scrappers on light tackle. We released over 30 fish and kept a few for the table. It was only 8:00 A.M. and our day was already a big success!

Fish and Move

Trolling is undoubtedly the most popular way of catching dolphin. Because you are covering a lot of ground, the chances of hooking dolphin, in addition to a variety of other species, increase considerably. However, many anglers don't have the patience or equipment to drag baits all day. If you fall into that category, it's time to try the run-and-gun approach!

Run-and-gun dolphin fishing is very simple in concept. First you cruise offshore, searching for birds, debris or weeds that might hold fish. After working one location, you pick up and look for the next target. The key is to keep moving until you find the fish. The technique is especially effective on those slow offshore days and on busy weekends, when you need to be the first one to fish these hot spots. However, while it appears very basic, there are several tricks to successful run-and-gun fishing.

Plan Your Route

My strategy involves designing the best possible course. For instance, I'll usually set an outer limit of 35 miles from my home port. Once we cross into the Gulf Stream, we'll keep our eyes open for any birds or floating objects, no matter how small. If we don't encounter any fish on the long haul, we'll cruise south about 10 miles before angling back inshore on a west/southwest heading. Then we'll head back toward our home port in a northerly fashion. Of course, we'll modify our course depending upon what we find, but it generally follows the same directional flow.

Providing that cloud cover doesn't interfere with satellite readings of the Earth, an updated chart of water-surface temperatures is invaluable. (Miami-based Roffer's Ocean Fishing Forecasting Service is one place to get this information.) Temperature changes often indicate a current edge where weedlines and debris accumulate. For instance, if there's a temperature change in an area 15 miles offshore (a one-degree change over a relatively short distance is considered significant off South Florida), we'll plan to run through the area. The precise edge of the Gulf Stream can also be determined by temperature readings. It's another good spot to look for dolphin-holding debris.

Flotsam Patrol

Any floating object, such as a jug, board, crate, tire or weed patch has the potential to hold fish. However, some will be more productive than others, and that's often determined by the amount of life around them. If you happen upon a weed line or scattered patches, look closely. If there are no baitfish, such as juvenile puffers, triggerfish and bar jacks, it's best to move on. Dolphin hang out around structure for food, so concentrate your efforts around objects that harbor lots of small fish.

It's the same with floating boards and other flotsam. If we happen upon one with no apparent signs of life, we'll fish it very quickly and then move on. If the piece of flotsam is holding bait, however, it gets a thorough inspection.

When a "floater" is surrounded by baitfish, that means it has been at sea long enough to establish a food-chain hierarchy. The growth accumulating on the flotsam sustains small fish, which in turn attract larger baitfish. And all that bait attracts dolphin.

Remember that flotsam often accumulates along the same current line. If a few objects or scattered weeds are located in one area, consider running along the line for several miles. The effort might yield additional targets.

Tackle Choices

Our run-and-gun tackle arsenal consists of three 12-pound-class spinning outfits, each rigged with a short (about two feet) Bimini twist and five feet of 30-pound monofilament leader. The double line and leader are joined by a surgeon's knot, with an Eagle Claw L256G 4/0 hook finishing off two of the rigs. The third outfit is rigged with a jig. We also keep two 20-pound-class spinning outfits rigged with 50-pound monofilament leaders and 5/0 hooks handy for large dolphin, and three eight-pound-class spinning outfits for schoolies. The light spinners are rigged with 12-pound leaders and either 3/0 hooks (for fishing bait), or jigs. We also carry a pair of lighter spinning outfits for catching live bait.

For bait and chum, we pack a few dozen ballyhoo, Spanish sardines, cigar minnows, pilchards, herring or mullet in a cooler. A five-pound box of small squid is frequently added to the menu, and we often carry a five-pound box of glass minnows or silversides, which make outstanding chum.

Fishing Floaters and Weed Lines

When we happen upon a floating target, we'll immediately fan-cast jigs around it. If a school turns up, we'll break out the light tackle and have some fun. If nothing happens, we'll vertical jig by free-spooling a lure 100 or so feet down and cranking it back to the surface. We also send a live bait or a bait chunk into the depths on a weighted 20-pound-test spinning outfit. In the interim, we'll "power chum" the target area with a few handfuls of cut bait and glass minnows. If nothing bites within 10 minutes, it's time to move on.

Weedlines require a slightly different approach. Compared to a single floating object that can be checked out within minutes, you need to work sections of a weedline. As in the method described earlier, edge up to a weed line and check for bait. If it appears promising, fan-cast jigs along the edge and begin chumming. And don't neglect to drop a jig or bait into the depths. If nothing happens, move on 200 feet or so and work another section of the weeds. Continue on in this fashion until you find the fish or reach the end of the weedline.

Another item that arouses deep-holding dolphin is a "chum bomb." Like the chum bombs used for yellowtail snapper, those that are used for dolphin are created by mixing pieces of cut bait or glass minnows with moist sand in a five-gallon bucket. Spicing the sand with menhaden oil is optional. Tightly pack a sand ball together in your hands, then drop it overboard. The weight of the sand rapidly carries the chum into the depths, releasing it as the ball breaks apart. The cloudy trail and the scent of the tasty morsels both serve to attract the dolphins' interest.

Live-Bait Resort

If dolphin are holding deep or are reluctant to eat the chunks or jigs, toss over a live bait. We usually catch our live bait from around the weeds and debris we find offshore. The trick is using bait-quill rigs, such as those made by Hayabusa, Owner and Mustad. Each rig has about six quills extending off a main leader. The lead end has either a swivel or a loop to attach it to the fishing line. Attach a small weight to the rig's opposite end. Simply drop the quill rig alongside the weeds or debris, let it sink 10 or 15 feet, then twitch it during a slow retrieve. The pulsating quills look like food to many small weed-line inhabitants, exactly what the dolphin are eating. Catching a few dozen baits is easy when they're thick, but don't become discouraged if you catch only a half dozen or so. Just let the baits swim in a five-gallon bucket and save them for those times when everything else fails.

Running-and-gunning for dolphin is as exciting as it is productive. That's because you're racing around the ocean looking for something that might lead you to fish. It's also very comfortable on those brutally hot days, since you're always generating a breeze as you move from spot to spot. One thing it isn't, however, is economical, so be prepared to spend some money on gas. But hopefully the fast action and tasty meals will far outweigh your expenses at the fuel pump!

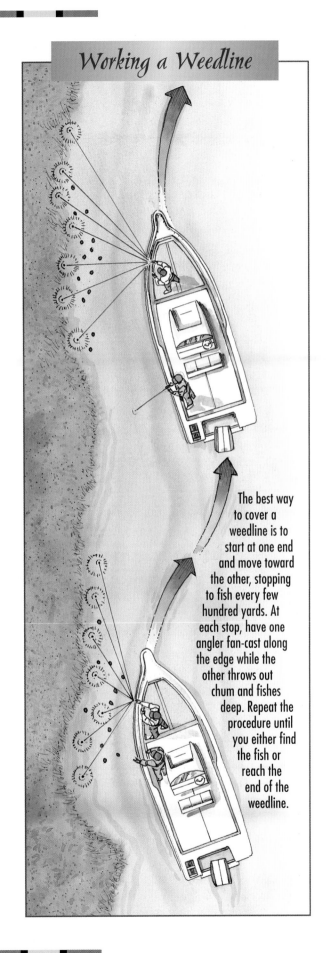

Working a Weedline

The best way to cover a weedline is to start at one end and move toward the other, stopping to fish every few hundred yards. At each stop, have one angler fan-cast along the edge while the other throws out chum and fishes deep. Repeat the procedure until you either find the fish or reach the end of the weedline.

Five Tricks for More Mahimahi

by Jim Rizzuto

Here are some clever tricks and techniques from Hawaiian charter captains that will help you catch more dolphin anywhere.

It's no secret that mahimahi (a.k.a. dorado or dolphin) gather around logs, coconuts, palm fronds, abandoned sections of net, derelict boats, fish-attracting buoys and even dead whales. But fishing these "floaters" can be a frustrating exercise. Along with the mahimahi, you'll often find a hungry horde of small fish capable of tearing your bait apart before the game fish can even see it. In tropical waters around the world, the spotted triggerfish – known in Hawaii as "hoggee" – swarm around floaters and will shred baits like piranhas. In this case, a "Charlie" can give you the edge by selectively drawing the mahimahi to your boat and away from the competitive hoggee.

Capt. Mike Stanford of the Kona-based *Howdy Do* makes his Charlies from dead skipjack tuna, also called aku. "If I have plenty of bait, I'll use a whole aku and just bridle it to a big-game hook and leader, live-bait style. But if I have only one or two aku, I'll slab out half of it and rig the carcass and the half in the same way."

Stanford puts the Charlie behind the boat about 50 to 60 feet back "at a spot where we can easily see the bait and anything that comes up on it," he says.

"We'll tow it at a knot or two around the floater, and the mahimahi will come up behind it and leave the hoggee behind. You go just slow enough so the Charlie glides under the surface and splashes once in a while. If there are any mahimahi around the floater, they will soon be behind the boat. It's the closest thing to an absolute guarantee I've ever seen."

Once the mahimahi show interest, Stanford rigs bait strips and feeds them back in the wake. "Depending on the circumstances, there are a couple of things you can do. If you have a lot of hoggee there, keep idling ahead and keep feeding strips back. The hoggee will go only so far away from the floater before turning back, but the mahimahi will come right to the boat. If the hoggee aren't there, you can put the boat in neutral and slowly bring the Charlie in while you are throwing baits back. You can usually lead them right up to the boat. That's when the action can be spectacular."

The aggressive mahimahi will try to pounce on the Charlie, too, but Stanford says it's important to keep it away from them. "If they take it, the action is over, and you'll end up with just one fish when you could have caught many. Still, you've got it rigged with a head hook just in case a big bull shows up. Then it's usually worth the sacrifice."

Big Baits Make Better Charlies

Capt. Rob Purdy of the *Puka Kai* advises choosing a big bait for a Charlie. "I'll take a five- to ten-pound skipjack because it's too big for the mahimahi to eat," says Purdy. "Also, big Charlies won't be damaged as much by the small mouths of the hoggees if you do get too close to the floater."

Purdy rigs his Charlies to a snap-swivel, not a hook, because he doesn't want to foul-hook a mahimahi that tries to eat it. "Put the Charlie line in an outrigger clip and run it up the rigger," Purdy advises. "This clears the area directly behind your boat to fight fish and allows the skipper to swing the boat around the Charlie while an angler is hooked up."

What if you find a floater, but don't have a skipjack for a Charlie? "Probably 80 percent or more floaters have some small yellowfin tuna [ahi] underneath," Stanford says. "If you don't have any bait and you are marking tuna down below, stop and drop down diamond jigs to pick up a few to use as baits. Be prepared for other fish, too. On one floater, recently, we also found a lot of wahoo, and got six or eight by deep-jigging with diamond jigs before we got our ahi bait. After we finally got the ahi, we slabbed it out and put it in the water. In no time we had a half dozen wahoo coming up on it. Then the mahimahi showed up and started eating. We also had some bigger ahi in the 30- to 40-pound class come up on it, and we got some of those too."

During some seasons, mahimahi are caught primarily on blind strikes by lure trollers. "Most of the time free-swimming mahimahi travel in twos or threes," Stanford says, "and only one may hit a lure. However, you can get the others if you're prepared to respond instantly. On the bridge I keep a light jig stick and 4/0 reel with 50-pound line. I also have leadered hooks and an ice chest with cut bait strips all set to go. If we get bit while trolling, I'll free-spool a strip back into the spread while the crewman is getting the lines cleared. From the bridge, I can control the strip and keep the lines from tangling. If there is another mahimahi around, we'll get him. During the course of the year, this doubles or triples the number of mahimahi we catch. Instead of getting just one fish, we get two, three or four, but it does take practice and preparation."

Purdy makes a science of preparing his strip baits. "I keep them in a sealable bag or plastic container so they aren't in direct contact with the ice. I cut my strips four to six inches long and a half inch wide, because neat strips make for a better presentation. Then I sprinkle them with sea salt to toughen them."

Purdy rigs his baits carefully so they won't tear off the hook if he needs to speed up or maneuver to deal with the fish that's already hooked. Rather than simply sticking the bait on a hook, he binds the leading end of the strip to the hook with a length of copper wire. This rig will remain intact at speeds of up to eight knots.

Stanford's favorite mahimahi hook is an 8/0 O'Shaughnessy extra-short shank, "the live-bait-style hook popular in Southern California," he says. Stanford prefers the Mustad 9175 (cadmium-plated), adding that "you can also get the extra-short shank in a beaked-point model, but they are not as easy to sharpen as the straight point."

Stanford leaders each hook with six feet of 80- or 130-pound-test monofilament. "When I fill a trolling reel from a bulk spool, there are usually a few hundred yards of line left over," Stanford says. "That's enough for a lot of leaders. You don't need a heavier leader if you change often. Mahimahi don't have sharp teeth, but they will wear through the monofilament in time."

Fooling with Lures

Mahimahi will frequently respond to the pop of a topwater chugging plug fished on a light casting rig, but few small lures have hooks that are strong enough to stand up to the fight. Therefore, Hawaiian mahimahi fishermen replace the light trebles with stronger double or single hooks. Stanford favors singles. "By the time you get a stainless steel double to a size that can hold a big fish, it's too big – it wrecks the action of the lure," he says.

To re-rig his poppers and diamond jigs he turns to his box of extra-short-shanked 8/0s. "I buy these by the box of a hundred so I can use them on everything," he says. They'll even hold the occasional 100-pound yellowfin that we sometimes get around the FAD buoys. This style has a wider gap and the extra strength you need. You can open up the eye with a crimping tool just enough to admit the wire of a plug or jig and then close it up with pliers."

Last-Resort Livies

Sometimes mahimahi won't respond to strip baits or lures. In this case, a live well stocked with goggle-eye scads or mackerel scads can save the day, but there is a trick to fishing them. When a live scad is dropped overboard, it will swim back to the boat and use the hull for protection. In its panic, it may even tangle your line and leader around the prop. "You could whack it on the head to stun it," says Capt. Juan Waroquiers of the *Illusions*, "but that defeats the purpose of using a live bait."

Another solution is to toss the bait far from the boat, but that can be difficult to do with a trolling rod. The solution? Strip 20 or 30 yards of line off the reel and coil it carefully on the deck. At this point, the hook end of the line is on the bottom of the pile and the reel end is on top. Pick the loops up and turn the coil over so that the hook end is on top. Now you should be able to toss the bait without fouling the loops. Just be ready for the strike, because the mahimahi will respond immediately to the splash of the bait.

Flies Match the Hatch

"Recently, I took out a fly fisherman and we fished around a small net where several boats were hooking mahi on bait," Capt. Purdy says. "We tried some flies that looked like small nehu [anchovies]. He hooked and landed several mahimahi and ono [wahoo] on the flies when no other artificial bait would work. I bought a dozen of the flies on the spot. I am amazed at how well they work. I use them for catching bait when the baitfish are hard to catch, but they catch everything else too. You don't need to fish them with a fly rod, but I was amazed at how hard mahimahi and ono fight on a nine weight!"

Hopefully all of the above tricks will help increase your catch of mahimahi, but it's important not to get carried away. Capt. Stanford's pet peeve is the uncaring angler who will decimate a school of small mahimahi. "It doesn't make any sense to take out an entire school of ten-pound mahimahi," he says. "They grow fast, and will be 20-pounders, soon enough. Have you ever caught a female that wasn't full of eggs? Give them a chance and there should be plenty of mahimahi for everyone."

Caution: Dangerous Dolphin

Part of catching mahimahi on lures is keeping them from catching you. Most mahimahi lures are rigged with more than one hook, and a wild mahimahi can inflict a lot of pain with those extra points. "I would rather gaff a 400-pound marlin than a 40-pound mahimahi," says Capt. Jack Ross, who has seen the havoc a mahimahi can wreak. "They take the prize for the most active of all game fish. They can hurt you even without getting close. Peter Budge was my crew one time when a mahimahi jumped next to the boat. The hooks pulled out and the lure flew back into the boat past our heads. A 10/0 hook went through Peter's arm. Luckily the barb was through and it was an easy removal, but from then on we've required shoes, shatterproof sunglasses and a low approach to gaffing."

What constitutes a "low approach" according to Capt. Ross? "When I bring a big mahimahi to gaff, as soon as I get the leader I have the angler place the rod in the chair holder and get in the cabin to stand clear. When leadering, I hold the leader low to the water and gaff the fish as I'm slowly pulling it into reach but before it comes to a stop. If I bring it to a stop first, all hell breaks loose and I'm going to have a very active time.

"I use a special gaff for mahimahi. The head is a 16/0 barbed hook screwed through the eye and wrapped on the handle. The barb helps make sure the fish stays on the gaff after it has been set. I have a 1/2-inch dowel crossbar on the end of the gaff at a right angle to the point to let me know exactly where the point is. I try to gaff the head to control the fish and then sweep — in one motion — the gaff, fish, and all into my fishbox.

"I make sure the lid is propped open beforehand with a stick or billy club, which is knocked out as the fish and gaff go in the box. That way, the lid slams shut. Also, if possible, I slide the lure up the leader to keep it out of the box and protect it from possible damage. Then I can disconnect the leader and have the angler sit on the lid of the box."

"A big mahimahi loose in the boat is nearly impossible to control. I've tried everything from covering the head with a burlap bag, striking the base of the tail with the club, grasping the mahi's head by the eye sockets, but nothing works all of the time. Charter skippers must go for safety first. That means controlling the fish, keeping people out of the way, and getting the fish into the fishbox. Congratulations and cameras come later. "

Windy-Weather Sharking

by Brion Babbitt

Charter pros use some special tricks to catch sharks consistently when the wind and seas kick up.

The ideal shark-fishing conditions for many anglers would probably include winds in the range of 10 to 15 knots – but anyone who has ever planned an ocean outing knows that things often turn out otherwise. However, if the gentle breeze you started the day with turns moderate, then fresh, and your boat is large enough to keep everyone safe and reasonably comfortable, there is absolutely no reason you can't successfully fish for sharks. Granted, you have to adjust your tactics to meet the new conditions, and Northeast captains who shark-fish day in and day out, over a wide range of wind and sea conditions, have figured out how to adapt without compromising their success.

Use a Sea Anchor

Aside from the obvious discomfort that fishing in nasty weather entails, the real problems with drift fishing for sharks in winds approaching 25 knots and over have to do with creating a chum slick and presenting the baits. To deal with the former, you need to slow down the speed of the drift, and the most effective way to do this is to use a sea anchor.

One veteran sharker who relies on a sea anchor is Captain Dan Guss of Cape May, New Jersey. "That's the only way you'll create a good slick, and the slick is the most important aspect of consistently attracting sharks," he says.

The sea anchor also stabilizes the vessel, Guss notes. The size of your boat, the wind resistance of its superstructure, the size of the sea anchor, and the anchor's position all affect the speed of drift. The cleat to which the sea anchor is tied determines the boat's angle to the seas.

Guss ties off his sea anchor amidships on his 44-foot boat, but John Williams, another New Jersey shark captain, places his a third of the boat length from the bow of his 40-footer. Different boats may need an alternative setup, even if the same type of sea anchor is used. The large-end diameter of Guss's sea anchor is five feet; William's is four. The object is not just to slow the boat's drift, but to keep it broadside to the sea so the lines can be evenly spaced.

Captain Neil McLaughlin, who fishes for sharks out of Delaware's Indian River Inlet, relies on sea anchors so much that he keeps three different sizes on his 38-foot charter boat. "I use a four-footer [diameter] in 18- to 20-knot winds, an eight-footer in 25 to 30 knots, and a 16-footer that I use when the winds get up around 35 knots," says McLaughlin. He also believes that the key to successful sharking is an unbroken, monolithic chum-line.

Anchor over Structure

Captain Mark Sampson out of Ocean City, Maryland, uses a sea anchor as well, but he also employs another fishing strategy that has proven quite successful. "I have a ten-foot-wide sea anchor that I use regularly on my 40-foot boat, but I also like to anchor rough bottom," says Sampson, who knows that uneven bottom is prime habitat for sharks. He likes to anchor because it keeps the bow facing into the seas, which makes it easier on his passengers.

After anchoring upcurrent from a productive looking piece of bottom, Sampson will suspend baits from beneath balloons and drift them back at different depths over the target area. One of the baits is drifted close to the bottom. To attract the sharks, Sampson will also chum heavily.

When a shark is hooked, Sampson attempts to fight the fish at anchor. However if it's a big fish he'll quickly add a large float to his rod and release from the anchor, much like chunk-fishing for bluefin tuna.

Add Weight, Chum Heavily

When winds are relatively calm at 10 to 12 knots, most sharkers fish a whole bait or fillet beneath a float with little or no additional weight. The length of line between the bait and float is adjusted to achieve the desired depth. But when winds accelerate to 20 knots or more, baits quickly rise in the water column, often far above the intended depth. They may also spin and dislodge the hook. This frequently results in twisted lines, snarled leaders and

frayed nerves. Also, lines fished from adjacent rods placed along the gunwale can tangle.

The solution is to add sinkers to the line. Most sharkers prefer to attach a heavy bank sinker or two below the end loop. Six to 16 ounces may be necessary to keep a two-pound Atlantic mackerel or bluefish fillet hanging vertically in the water column. A bait that's fished deeper than 75 feet may require even more weight

Captain Phil Lewis, who fishes the waters off Montauk, New York, doesn't use a sea anchor in heavy seas, but chums more heavily than normal and adds plenty of lead to achieve the proper bait depth. He fishes only two or three lines from his 36-foot boat in heavy, wind-blown seas to prevent tangling problems. Lewis clearly remembers the 600-pound mako he caught in 30-knot northeast winds and tall waves. Extra-heavy chumming and ample weight did the job to capture that trophy.

Live Baits and Kites

Another productive technique Lewis employs doesn't require the use of floats or weights. "I like to fish a live bluefish topside," says Lewis, "even in rough seas, just hook the fish in front of the dorsal fin, but don't penetrate the spine."

Serious sharkers agree that live bluefish are prime shark food, with the bonus that they can be fished shallow without the need for additional weight. Sharkers rely on the swimming, splashing attraction of a live blue to get strikes rather than its precise positioning below the surface.

Sampson also takes advantage of high winds to present a live bluefish from a kite, a technique that produces sharks as well as other species of game fish. "Another big plus is that the kite puts a bait on the leeward side of the boat, away from the drifting float lines on the windward side," says Sampson, who has kites for light, medium, heavy and extra-heavy winds.

Captain Jeff Pickens works his 35-footer in the same Montauk waters as Lewis. Pickens has used as much as 20 ounces of lead to force the bait down deep in rolling waves. Pickens considers riding three- to six-foot waves a "normal ocean" for his shark trips. However, he doesn't use a sea anchor, since he wants to cover six to seven miles in about four hours of drift time.

"It's important to use more chum when it's windy, and to partially thaw the frozen, ground-up bunker chum before using it to thicken the slick," Pickens advises. He finds that three shark rods are about all he can manage in a big sea, but keeps a fourth rod baited and ready in the cockpit for critters that show at boatside without warning.

In heavy seas, Pickens runs one drift line to an outrigger clip, which is hung from a short length of line, attached to the bow. This widens the spread of his lines and decreases the chance of a tangle.

Windy-day sharking may not be for everyone. And while a change in shark-fishing tactics can't improve the weather, it can turn the odds distinctly in your favor.

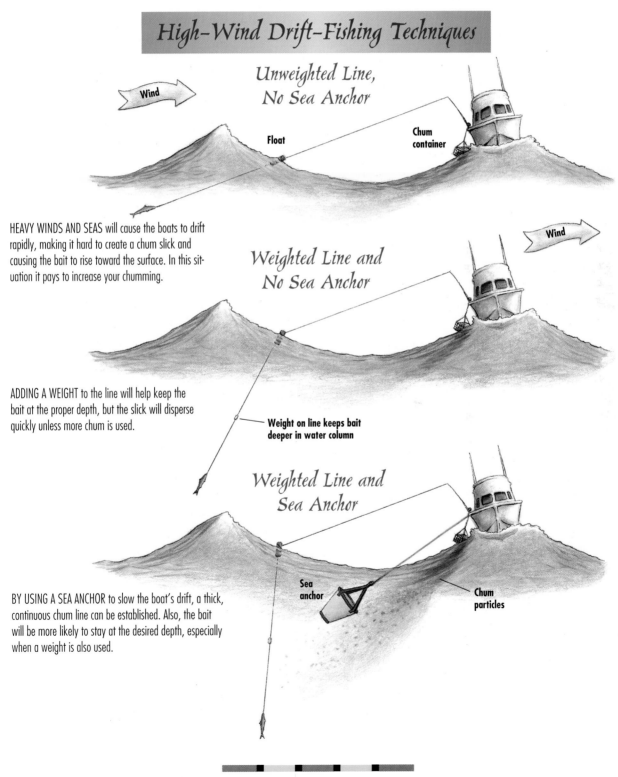

High-Wind Drift-Fishing Techniques

Unweighted Line, No Sea Anchor

Wind

Float

Chum container

HEAVY WINDS AND SEAS will cause the boats to drift rapidly, making it hard to create a chum slick and causing the bait to rise toward the surface. In this situation it pays to increase your chumming.

Weighted Line and No Sea Anchor

Wind

ADDING A WEIGHT to the line will help keep the bait at the proper depth, but the slick will disperse quickly unless more chum is used.

Weight on line keeps bait deeper in water column

Weighted Line and Sea Anchor

Sea anchor

Chum particles

BY USING A SEA ANCHOR to slow the boat's drift, a thick, continuous chum line can be established. Also, the bait will be more likely to stay at the desired depth, especially when a weight is also used.

Blue Shark

Be a Better Shark Chummer

by Brion Babbitt

Expert sharkers reveal some special tricks to get the action going in the slick.

Successfully attracting sharks on a regular basis demands more than simply soaking a bucket of chum. Variable ocean and wind conditions won't guarantee effective drift-chumming or, in reality, any drift at all. Add to this a few evolving theories on just what gets a toothy predator to take a bait and you'll understand why top East Coast skippers are constantly developing new ways to attract and catch sharks.

Jump-Start Your Slick

Savvy sharkers have discovered a novel technique for getting the action started quickly. Before setting up for a drift, they slow to bluefish trolling speed or slightly slower. Then, using the washdown hose, a crew member will direct water into a chum can, washing oil and meat particles overboard in a continuous trail.

Heikki Poolake, a small-boat sharker from South Jersey, puts his "jump-start" chum can in the splashwell of his 22-foot twin outboard. Professional sharker Capt. Billy Verbanas of Indian River Inlet, Delaware – whose boat holds the Delaware state mako record at 942 pounds – places his first chum can near a transom scupper on his 40-footer while he power-chums. Verbanas jump-starts his slick for at least a half-mile before settling into standard drift-chumming. Without this tactic, Verbanas says,

it usually takes up to two hours to establish a slick that's long enough to begin drawing sharks.

Power Drifting

Every sharker has had a perfect morning breeze die and leave a flat, windless sea. With no wind or current to push the boat, chum particles sink uselessly straight down. However, you can extend your chum slick by starting an engine, moving the boat ahead 50 yards or so, then shutting down again. But watch your speed. The shark floats tend to pull together into a line under power, causing the baits to tangle if you go too fast. Repeat the power-drifting process to gradually work out more chum and cover new territory.

Tournament winner Capt. Dan Guss of New Jersey, says he's salvaged plenty of windless trips by power drifting on his 40-foot *Huntress*. "I drag my chum bucket while bumping the boat in and out of gear," reveals Guss, a serious sharker with 32 years experience and a 542-pound mako to his credit.

Poolake uses another trick on his 22-footer. If the wind dies he pulls out an electric trolling motor, puts it between the outboards on a homemade plywood mounting bracket, and he's off! He concedes that the trolling motor can't match the drift generated by a good 10- to 15-knot wind, but it beats sitting still in a pool of bunker oil.

clipped a shark leader rigged with a whole mackerel to the bird's rear snap. After drifting the bird into the slick, just as he would an ordinary shark float, he began retrieving it erratically using short upward sweeps of the rod tip, occasionally resting the teaser between sweeps.

The teaser splashed and sputtered. After cranking the bird all the way back to the boat, he free-spooled it back into the slick and repeated the drill. After ten minutes of "teasing," a blue shark charged past three subsurface baits suspended by floats and struck the bird bait.

Moral? While sharks do feed by smell, a natural bait embellished with noise and topwater action may be even more appealing.

Bait Presentation

Makos are fast-moving animals with high metabolism, but that's not true of all shark species. Blue sharks, for example, have a markedly slower metabolism. I've watched blue sharks ignore a spread of subsurface baits when tracking chum scent to the boat, then refuse typical whole-fish baits and fillets.

Mako Shark

Finding Sharks

Most shark experts plan a course that involves drifting over rapidly changing bottom contours or structure. That's a proven strategy. But there's another tactic you can use, although it's a matter of opportunity. On your way to the shark grounds, keep an eye out for schools of surface-feeding fish. If you find bluefish, bonito, skipjacks, mackerel or any other fish creating a topwater ruckus, you've likely found sharks. Where fish splash and flash, sharks lurk below. I've located many species, from makos and blues to hammerheads and tigers, by simply shutting down and chumming near this type of surface commotion. Bear in mind, however, that a handful of forage fish won't cut it; look for large, noisy schools that really ring the dinner bell.

Topwater Shark Teaser

"Watch this," said Capt. Ray Szulczewski of Cape May, New Jersey. He snapped a Boone Bird tuna teaser to the swivel on his 50-pound line, then

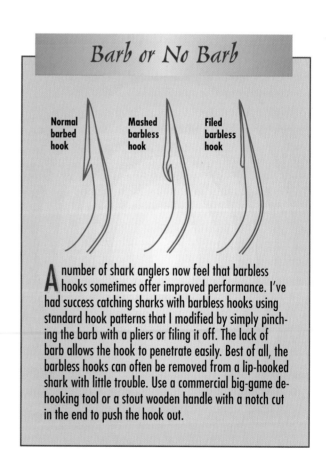

Barb or No Barb

Normal barbed hook

Mashed barbless hook

Filed barbless hook

A number of shark anglers now feel that barbless hooks sometimes offer improved performance. I've had success catching sharks with barbless hooks using standard hook patterns that I modified by simply pinching the barb with a pliers or filing it off. The lack of barb allows the hook to penetrate easily. Best of all, the barbless hooks can often be removed from a lip-hooked shark with little trouble. Use a commercial big-game de-hooking tool or a stout wooden handle with a notch cut in the end to push the hook out.

The problem is bait size. Often, a blue that refuses a one-pound mackerel will readily gulp down smaller chunks of the same offering, especially if the tidbit is presented on a small hook.

Sharks can also be bait-type selective. Once, after fishing mackerel baits all day without a strike, I tried a fresh bonito fillet on one of the rods. The new bait was attacked in seconds. After releasing that shark, I re-baited with another bonito fillet, which was instantly struck by another blue shark that had evidently been lurking beneath the boat.

Big Baits, Big Makos

"If a big mako shows up, throw a mackerel fillet off each side of the boat right away," Capt. Billy Verbanas instructed his crew during a recent shark trip to Poorman's Canyon. "That'll keep him interested until we get the baits in." Large makos can be impatient, and Verbanas wasn't taking any chances after investing 20 hours in a chum slick that now stretched for miles. The slick had already produced more than a dozen huge blue sharks and a 285-pound longfin mako.

Three hours later, at 1:30 A.M., a massive mako swam into the spreader lights. Mate Dan Devine instantly responded with the appetizer, then presented the main course – a big, double-hooked fillet from a 20-pound bluefin tuna, served up on an 80-pound-class, bent-butt outfit. Forty-five minutes later a 660-pound mako lay in the cockpit.

Giant makos that inhabit the Atlantic canyons and beyond dine on big forage fish, including small tunas and swordfish. Small, whole fish or strip baits, which are fine in 20 and 30 fathoms for 50- to 125-pound makos, just don't cut it. In water over 100 fathoms, the best baits are jumbo fillets or long chunks, which ensure that an outsized mako gets something to chew on before making up its mind to leave.

It doesn't hurt to be prepared when sharking in shallower waters, either. Many experienced captains who rarely fish for sharks in water deeper than 30 fathoms keep a fresh four- or five-pound bluefish rigged with two hooks for the occasional fat mako. Remember, you won't have time to rig one if a trophy fish suddenly shows!

Quick-Rig Blue Shark Leader

To make a simple, economical blue shark leader, crimp a loop in one end of 15 feet or more of 400 or 480-pound-test stainless steel cable. This will serve as a reusable "butt" section of the leader. Then crimp a 250-pound-test ball bearing snap swivel to the other end.

Haywire a Mustad #7731 9/0 or Mustad #7754 10/0 hook to four feet of 175- or 250-pound-test single-strand wire, and haywire a loop in the other end. Prepare two dozen of these short (about three feet when finished) "mini-leaders" beforehand. Then, after releasing the first blue shark (assuming you've chosen to cut the single-strand leader), just unclip the remaining piece and snap on a fresh one.

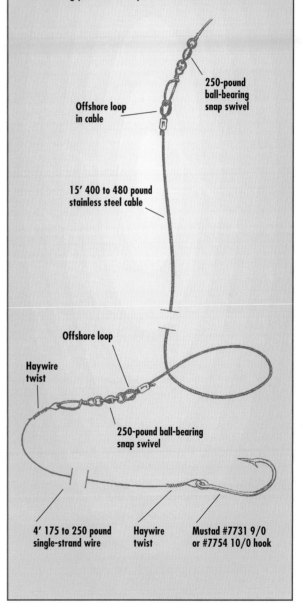

250-pound ball-bearing snap swivel

Offshore loop in cable

15' 400 to 480 pound stainless steel cable

Offshore loop

Haywire twist

250-pound ball-bearing snap swivel

4' 175 to 250 pound single-strand wire

Haywire twist

Mustad #7731 9/0 or #7754 10/0 hook

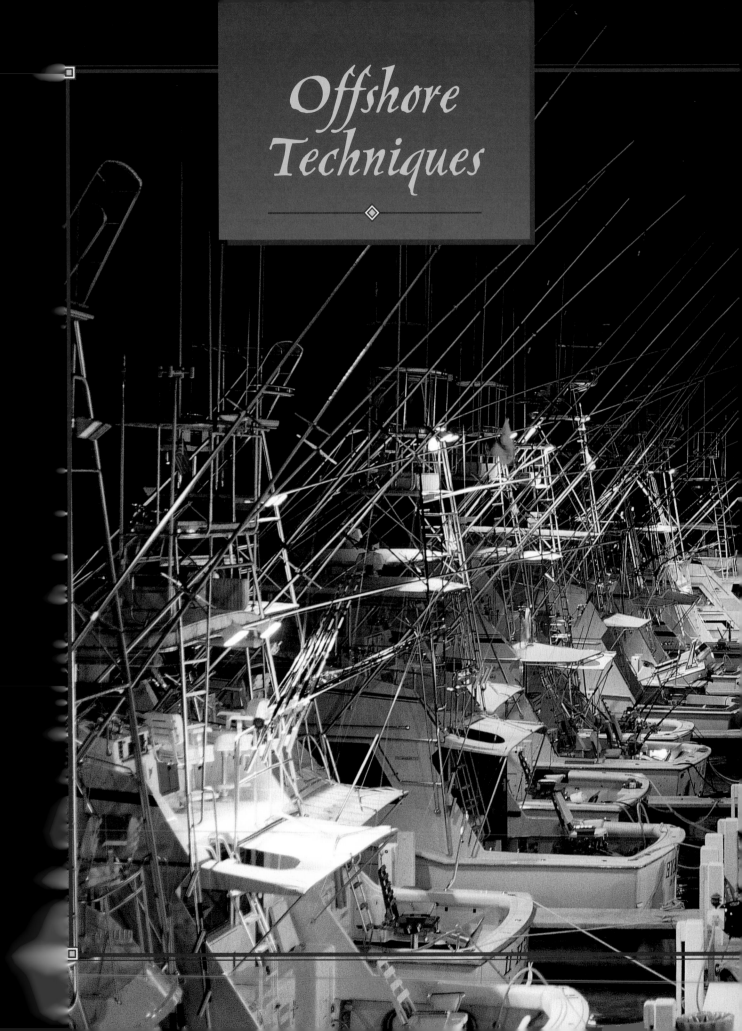

Offshore
Techniques

WALKER'S CAY, BAHAMAS

OFFSHORE TECHNIQUES:

Beat 'Em with Braids

by Mike Moore

The new generation of smaller two-speed reels filled with superlines are giving anglers the edge over the world's largest — and smartest — gamefish.

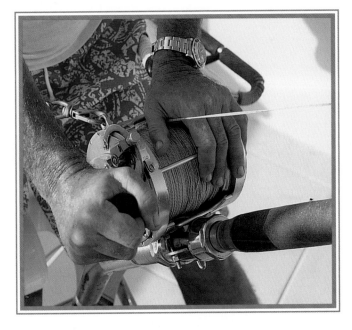

The hot sun beat down upon the fishermen aboard the long-range sportfisher *Royal Polaris* as huge yellowfin tuna darted through the cobalt water below the boat. The bite was spotty, with the majority of fish turning up their noses at the live baits, but the few tuna that had been landed were massive. Just as everyone's patience was starting to wear thin, Stas Vellonakis grabbed his souped-up International 16S and flipped out a live sardine. Because the reel was filled with 80-pound Spectra "super-braid" connected to a short section of 60-pound monofilament, the bait sped into turbo drive and soon captured the attention of a hungry yellowfin. One hour later, the 287-pound tuna was gaffed aboard.

It was a major feat to land such a huge fish on light tackle from an anchored boat, but Vellonakis's gear had made it possible. It was just one example of how the new generation of braided lines and specialized reels are helping long-range anglers – and others – hook and land the biggest and wariest fish that swim. Much of it boils down to being able to fish small live baits with as little resistance as possible. This is where today's super-braid line comes in. Because braid is ultrathin, it offers less resistance than monofilament, which makes it easier for small-sized

bait to swim around. Line drag hinders a bait's swimming ability and makes it look unnatural, resulting in fewer strikes.

Another major advantage of super-braid is its lack of stretch, which allows the fisherman to feel his bait's every move. This makes it easy to tell when the bait needs to be changed or is about to be eaten. Less stretch and resistance also equates to more positive hook sets, which can be significant with hard-jawed predators such as wahoo, kingfish and billfish, or big bottom feeders such as halibut, grouper or yellowtail.

While braided line is the key to fishing small live baits, monofilament (and fluorocarbon) still has its place as a leader or "top shot," since it's less visible than braid. Monofilament also acts as a shock absorber, which can prevent pulled hooks. The system works like this: after the reel is filled to about ¾ capacity with super-braid, a wind-on monofilament or fluorocarbon leader is connected to the braid via a loop-to-loop connection. An alternative is to connect a longer monofilament or fluorocarbon top shot directly to the braid with a knot or crimp. For example, on bright, sunny days when the fish are acting shy, I often rig a 40-foot top shot of 60- to 130-pound fluorocarbon.

More Line, Less Waste

Superline also has allowed anglers to use small to medium-sized lever-drag reels on big-game species thanks to its small diameter. According to John Rowe of Izorline International, a distributor of Spectra braid, 80-pound Spectra has roughly the same diameter as 25-pound monofilament. This means that anglers can pack more line on a reel without sacrificing strength. Furthermore, superline users will benefit from reduced waste during line changes, since only the short forward section of monofilament needs to be dumped. Spectra line costs more, but will pay for itself over time.

When it comes to taking on big fish with small reels, you can't cut corners. Insist on a sturdy lever-drag model that has the guts to deliver 20 to 40 pounds of drag, yet can also be placed in complete free-spool for casting small baits. Accurate Products is one of the few manufacturers whose reels meet these requirements right out of the box. The company now markets a full line of lever-drag reels equipped with drag washers on each side of the spool. The Platinum TDR 6, 12, 30, 50, and 50 wide offer high and low gears, plus total free-spool with drag settings up to 50 pounds. Similar in size to a Penn 16S, the 30 TDR will hold about 500 yards of 80-pound superline, plus a 100-yard top shot of 60-pound monofilament.

Other two-speed reels used for serious stand-up work include models from Penn and Shimano. Popular Shimano reels include the TLD 20, 30 and 50. These reels cast well and deliver smooth free-spool with drag settings of 19 to 25 pounds.

Also popular on the long-range front are the Penn International 12T, 16S, 30T and 50S, although they don't deliver the complete free-spool needed to cast small baits with heavy drag settings. Fortunately, California engineer Cal Sheets offers a solution for Penn users. Sheets can beef up the drag (also called "blueprinting"), convert the reels to two-speed (if necessary), and install upgraded casting bearings to improve casting distance.

Critical Drag

When it comes to handling big fish on these smaller reels, proper drag setting is a must. Skipper Randy Toussaint of the *Royal Star* offers some important insight on this matter. "With superlines, it's crucial to use less drag on the strike because of the lack of stretch. When a big fish takes off on its first run, it's easy for that surge to snap the line. I like to see anglers use at least 100 yards of monofilament top shot with an initial drag setting of about 18 to 20 pounds (figuring 80-pound braid combined with a top shot of 60-pound monofilament). I also like to see the fish take lots of line on its first run. If a big yellowfin goes straight down early in the fight, you're in trouble, and it generally turns into a wind-and-grind battle."

Fellow captain Tim Ekstrom adds that it's important to pack superline on the spool very tightly to prevent it from digging into itself under heavy drag pressure. "It's super-slick stuff, so be ready to back off on the drag in a hurry. You won't hear the kind of crackling sound that monofilament makes when it's cutting into itself. However, there is a time and a place to push the drag to full, and that's when a big fish settles into a fighting circle. The weight of a 200-pound tuna circling at color often pulls line off the spool, even with 30 pounds of drag. If there's a swell running, the extra drag really pays off. Remember, you've got to have enough drag to keep moving a fish toward the boat, even if it's only a couple of inches at a time.

Safety First!

If you practice catch-and-release, getting the fish to the boat quickly with the aid of a heavy drag bodes well for its survival. But before you lock down the drag, consider the dangers of bringing a "hot" fish to the boat. I recently battled a 150-pound yellowfin to gaff in just five minutes aboard the *Qualifier 105*, but was nearly pulled over the side when a foiled gaff attempt sent the fish screaming for the bottom. Luckily, the deckhands dropped their gaffs and grabbed my legs, possibly saving my life. The lesson? Always pay close attention to your drag setting, and keep a sharp cutting device on your person.

Braided line, combined with today's reel technology, is giving bait fishermen a measure of confidence that was often missing in the past. So the next time you're faced with a seemingly impossible group of fussy game fish, maximize your chances by casting baits on the braid. When combined with a good two-speed reel, braided line could be the best fishing investment you ever make.

Crimp

Mono threaded inside braided line

200-pound super-braid or Dacron

Spliced loop

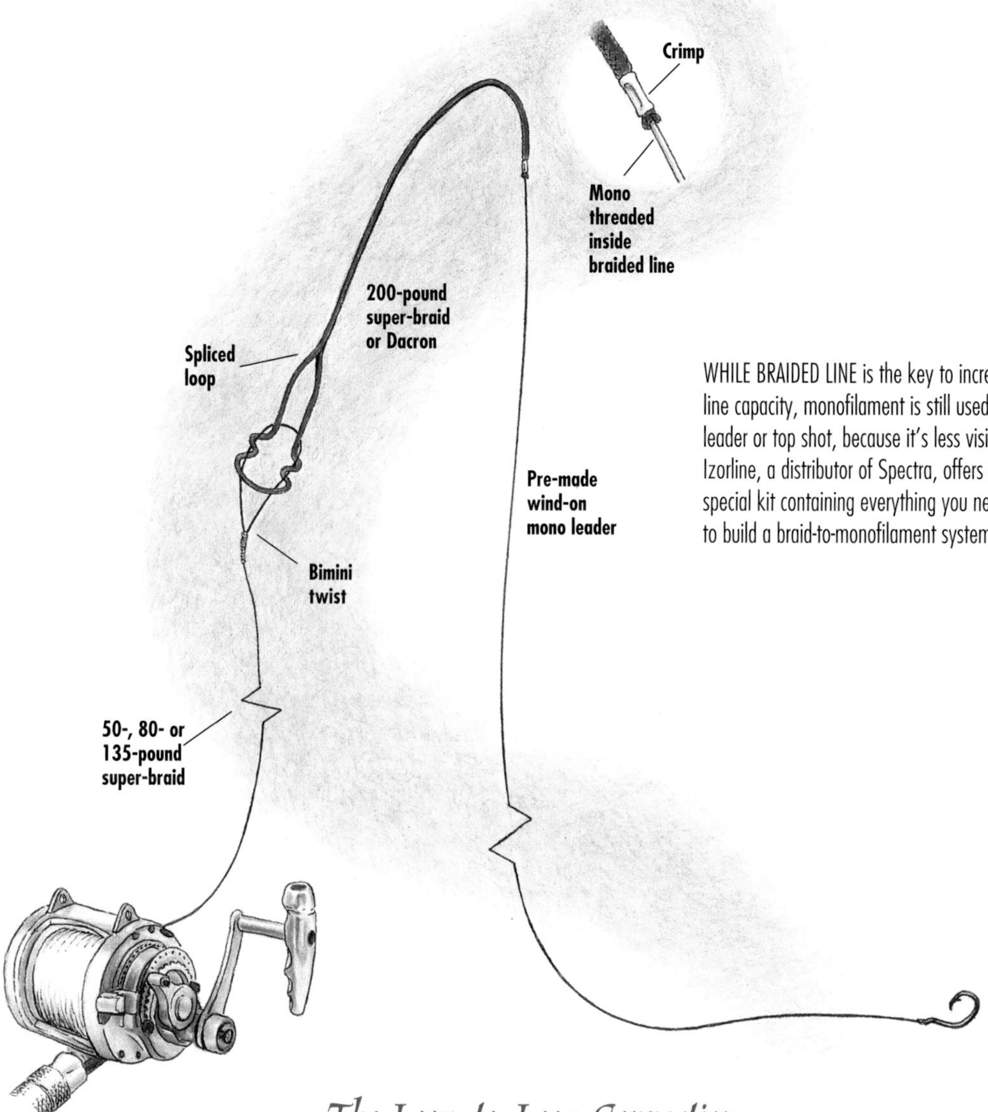

WHILE BRAIDED LINE is the key to increased line capacity, monofilament is still used as a leader or top shot, because it's less visible. Izorline, a distributor of Spectra, offers a special kit containing everything you need to build a braid-to-monofilament system.

Bimini twist

Pre-made wind-on mono leader

50-, 80- or 135-pound super-braid

The Loop-to-Loop Connection

Bimini twist

1. Pass superline Bimini loop through the loop of the wind-on leader. Bimini should have 40 twists.

WIND ON LEADER

2. Pass the wind-on spool through the superline loop.

3. Pull ends gently to line up the loops. Leave enough room for the wind-on spool.

WIND ON LEADER

4. Pass the wind-on spool through both loops 2 to 4 times.

5. Slowly and evenly pull the ends apart, bringing the loops together.

6. The finished loop-to-loop connection.

Catch Your Own Live Baits

by George Poveromo

Professional South Florida bait supplier, Ray Mendez, shares his secrets for consistently finding and catching goggle–eyes, pilchards and other live baits for his customers to use in catching sailfish and other offshore denizens.

A light chop fueled by an easterly breeze gently rocked the boat as Ray Mendez shut down in 400 feet of water off Ft. Lauderdale. After checking his position and dousing the cabin lights, Mendez moved to the cockpit and began the task of deploying three 12-foot rods, each rigged with long strings of tiny bait quills that would be positioned at different depths. The target of this nocturnal endeavor was the much coveted goggle-eye, a favorite offering among South Florida sailfishermen and one of several bait species that Mendez has made it his business to catch.

Full moons can be a handicap when catching bait, according to Mendez, so he had us on the water right after sunset. During the full-moon stages, he explained, the best bite is often early, generally between sunset and 10:00 P.M. "There's also a good bite just before sunrise," Mendez continued as he eyed the rods, the tips of which were wrapped with bands of yellow tape for visibility. "That's often the case, but certainly not law. You just never know. There have been times when I haven't caught bait under ideal conditions, and other times when I've loaded up when the conditions were all wrong."

Mendez's experience paid off on this occasion, and his long bait rods were soon dipping under the strain of goggle-eyes that had eaten the quills in approximately 250 feet of water. When the bite is hot and heavy, it doesn't take him long to fill a large live well, especially when he's fishing 16 hooks per rig!

A supplier of live goggle-eyes and pilchards to sport fishermen around South Florida's Port Everglades Inlet, Mendez has been operating his now-famous blue-hulled vessel, *Ray's Live Bait*, for over six years. He enjoys a devoted clientele, and business has been brisk enough to support a second boat. Part of the reason for his success is Mendez's ability to provide baitfish for his customers on a regular basis, something that many recreational fishermen wish they could do on their own. Which is precisely why I had sought his advice.

Go Deep for Goggles

One little-known secret of Ray's is that goggle-eyes can be caught in relatively deep water at night, and not necessarily over structure, such as deep wrecks or reefs. Off the South Florida coast, he prefers drifting to locate bait, covering a broad depth zone ranging from 80 to 400 feet of water.

"The depth basically depends on the area I'm fishing," he says. "Off Palm Beach, the 40- to 80-foot zone can be very good, while in other areas it's the 150- to 250-foot zone that's most productive. As a general rule, if you drift between 200 feet and the reefs, you should catch all the goggle-eyes you'll need."

Ray always shuts down the engine when he's drifting for goggle-eyes, and prefers to keep things dark on board. Also, he doesn't use chum to attract the fish and get them feeding, and points out that the goggle-eyes will often gather beneath the boat as it drifts along.

Because of the depth and the quantity of bait needed, his gear consists of three 12-foot rods with Penn Senator 4/0 reels spooled with 40-pound monofilament. His favorite goggle-eye rigs are the Hayabusa D-119 (eight quills), D115 (six white quills) and D-155 (eight-hook rig with pink and white quills). He'll often double the number of quills by connecting a second rig to the first. To keep the rigs positioned at the desired depths, and to prevent the baits from tangling, a 16- to 32-ounce sinker is attached to the end.

If he's not marking bait on the fishfinder, Ray positions his deep rig at 100 feet. The mid-depth rig is fished at 80 feet, whereas the shallow rig is set at 40 feet. The rods are spread out along the gunwale

and left in holders, with the rocking motion of the boat providing the action.

Once a concentration of goggle-eyes is located, the water depth and position of the quill rig is noted, which helps narrow the search area. If one portion of the water column is more active, the other rigs are adjusted accordingly. "I drift between 30 and 45 minutes before repositioning," says Ray. "That's usually ample time to cover enough ground, and for a school of bait to start collecting under the boat.

"These fish are moving around, so it's a matter of finding them. As a very general rule, goggle-eyes hold offshore at night and gradually move to the reefs and beaches during the early-morning hours. They seem to disappear and get lockjaw during the day. I have no idea where they go. Covering the different depth zones is important. Experiment. I've had nights when the goggle-eyes bit great in 160 feet of water, just off the bottom."

Mendez contends that the best bait bite occurs between midnight and dawn, no matter what the moon phase. There are exceptions, of course, particularly around the full moon, when the goggle-eyes seem more active between sunset and 10:00 P.M. "Feeding patterns develop over time," says Ray. "If I've been catching goggle-eyes during the late bite two or three nights in a row and they suddenly stop eating the next night, I'll try fishing for them earlier." However, he stresses that if you fish hard between 4:00 A.M. and sunrise, you'll often gather enough goggle-eyes, pilchards, runners and speedos for a day of fishing, regardless of moon phase.

Mendez also reveals that bait can be caught around large ships and freighters that anchor offshore. During the evening and early-morning hours, quill rigs should be cast around the upcurrent sides of these vessels, where the goggle-eyes will be schooling underneath the hull, facing into the current. Sometimes the bait will school up tight to the ship, while other times they'll hold 40 to 60 feet away and close to the bottom. If the upcurrent end of the ship isn't producing, broaden your search to include the entire shadow line, and always watch for bait schools on the fishfinder. If the bait's there, but not feeding, fish elsewhere and try again later. They may turn on.

If the deep-water approach fails to produce, Mendez will move inshore. Like many anglers, he knows that navigational aids and mooring buoys are

Goggle-eye (top),
Pilchard (below)

notorious bait hangouts, as are reef lines, small wrecks and other prominent structure. It's at these spots that Mendez will anchor and deploy a frozen block of chum.

"There have been times when the deep water has failed, and I must rely on coming in shallow and anchoring on structure," he says. "This is when I'll chum, and I'll catch goggle-eyes, speedos, pilchards and blue runners. The buoys and markers are ideal spots to catch your own bait, since they're easy to find. In fact, you should be able to catch all the bait you'll need between 4:00 A.M. and sunrise."I set the rigs near bottom, place the rods in holders and let the motion of the boat provide the action. If the action is spotty, I recommend fishing the buoys and markers when the sun comes up for blue runners, speedos and bullet bonito."

Pilchard Patrol

Mendez also searches for pilchards at night. His technique involves tying off to a mooring buoy or anchoring along a reef line in 15 to 45 feet of water and dispensing a block of chum. He'll first look for bait on the fishfinder, the schools appearing as light scratches because they're spread out at night. If the current is strong he'll fish the shallower zones.

Some anglers use lights to attract bait, but Mendez opts for total darkness. He says that the pilchards will swim right up to the chum bag, enabling him to "dip-fish" his quill rigs. His pilchard rig is nothing more than an Owner model 5553-037 No. 8 quill rig tied to one foot of household twine, which is tied to the tip of a short cane pole. Using this simple setup, he lowers the quill rig behind the chum bag and waits for the fish to jump on. There's no twitching or any other action imparted to the quills, which are left to dangle in the current.

Mendez usually catches one or two pilchards at a time, and uses a small de-hooker to drop each bait into the live well. Care is taken not to touch the bait, which removes their protective coating of slime. The same applies to goggle-eyes.

Goggle-eyes and pilchards are prime live baits off South Florida and the Keys. Both species are regularly lowered to the bottom for grouper, snapper and cobia; drifted and slow-trolled for sailfish, king mackerel, bonito, blackfin tuna, wahoo and dolphin; and even used for sight casting to dolphin and sailfish. Knowing how to catch your own share of fresh and frisky livies will give you a decided edge the next time you head offshore.

Catch More with a Kite!

by John Brownlee

A Florida Keys pro gives his tips on how to maximize your fishing time with kites.

One of the best things about kite fishing is that you frequently get to see the strike. A recent trip off the Florida Keys serves as a good example. We had been fishing for several hours without any action, when the two pilchards that were dangling from our kite suddenly became terrified by something below and began swimming in circles on the surface.

Such behavior signals the presence of a predator, and sure enough, two sailfish appeared beneath the baits and engulfed the pilchards simultaneously. When the fish felt the hook they headed off in opposite directions, jumping frantically and shaking their heads. Such scenes make an offshore fisherman's trip!

We might have caught the sails on free-lined baits, of course, but the kite made it much more exciting, and may have even helped entice the fish to eat in the first place. That's because kites allow you to keep most or all of your terminal tackle out of the water, so fish see less of the hook, leader and knots. Instead, they focus on the thrashing baitfish.

While sailfish are the species most closely associated with kite fishing, they are by no means the only fish you can catch using this versatile technique. Tunas, dolphin, wahoo, king mackerel, cobia and even tarpon (yes, tarpon) can all be caught with the aid of kites at one time or another. Basically, any fish that likes live bait presented near the surface can be taken with a kite.

Setting Up a Kite Rig

For those of you who are unfamiliar with kite fishing, let's go over some basics. A specialized fishing kite is flown from the boat with several release clips attached at intervals along the kite line. The fishing lines are snapped into the clips as the kite is let out, thereby taking the baits the desired distance from the boat. The fishing line goes up to the clip, then straight down to the water. (A solid ring is sometimes placed on the fishing line to minimize abrasion and to keep the line from tangling in the clip.)

By paying close attention and adjusting the line, you can keep the bait on the surface, where it makes a commotion that predators often find irresistible. Furthermore, instead of lying in the water, where a fish might see it, your leader hangs in the air above the baitfish, out of sight.

Kite rods are stumpy versions of fishing rods with one or two guides, and the release clips are usually Black's outrigger clips that have been pre-drilled with various-size holes in them. Swivels are tied into the kite line, which is often made of Dacron because it cuts the wind better. A small swivel is placed nearest the kite, followed by a larger swivel.

The first release clip (the one closest to the boat) has a large enough hole to slide over the smaller swivel, so it can be reeled in with the line, while the second, larger swivel keeps it from sliding down the line when deployed. The release clip closest to the kite has a smaller hole and is held in place by the first swivel. If you don't want to deal with swivels, a company called DuBro makes a release clip that simply snaps onto the kite line wherever you want to put it (right). Lots of captains are switching to this clip because it lets you alter the spacing of your baits to match the conditions, and you eliminate the use of swivels entirely.

DuBro release clip

Conventional wisdom has the clips spaced about 60 feet apart. That's open to individual interpretation, of course, but 60 feet seems to be close enough to keep the baits relatively near one another, yet far enough apart to keep them from tangling. Long leaders (ten feet plus) are the norm, and most people place a marker of some sort where the leader and double line meet so they can tell how deep the bait is. Fluorescent surveyor's tape and small orange floats work well as markers, and be sure to use a quality ball-bearing snap swivel between the leader and double line, because the baits swim in circles lots of times, which can turn your line into a twisted mess in no time.

That's a very general description of kite fishing, which is something of an art form. To learn more, we asked Captain Randy Towe of Tavernier, Florida to give us some tips on kite-fishing strategy. Randy is a Florida Keys guide who happens to be proficient at both flats and offshore fishing. He does the latter in his 31-foot Contender, *Quit Yer Bitchin'*, and he spends a lot of his time fishing with kites.

Fly It Quiet

Randy fishes kites while drifting, but also uses them at anchor if current and/or wind carry him out of his preferred depth range. "The ideal situation is drifting with the engines off, so everything's quiet," Randy says. "A good drift is 45 minutes to an hour where I can stay in the general water depth I want to be in. The current is the real key."

For example, when sailfishing, you normally want to be just off the reef line in 80 to 200 feet of water. If the wind and current allow you to drift parallel to the reef, keeping you in the same relative depth, you're in good shape. But when the wind blows hard perpendicular to the reef, you may end up too shallow or too deep, so anchoring in your chosen depth is the way to go.

In a normal spread, Randy fishes two lines off the kite and a couple of flat lines. Many captains use kites to take the baits far away from the boat, but Randy likes them closer. "I fish my kite baits close together, with the first swivel 25 feet from the kite and another 25 feet below that," Randy explains. "This setup increases the number of double hook ups, but it also means you have to pay very close attention to the baits to keep them from tangling."

Randy also doesn't hesitate to put a second kite up if the first kite is out-producing the flat lines. He keeps the kites separated by crimping a large split shot to the outside corners of the two kites. The weight makes the kites fly off to one side, away from each other. You can also run the kite lines through

A GOGGLE-EYE rigged for kite fishing.

your outrigger pins and out to the end of the 'riggers to separate the kites even more.

Favorite kite baits in South Florida include goggle-eyes, blue runners, pilchards and cigar minnows. "The main thing about bait presentation is to make them look natural," Randy says. "The better a bait looks to you, the better it looks to a fish."

Many Florida kite fishermen attach their baits to the hooks via bridles, but Towe likes to hook them lightly through the back. "Hooking baits in the back has brought us just as much success as bridling, and it's much faster," he explains. "If you could prove to me that bridling keeps the baits from spinning and will improve my hook up ratio, then I'd be all for it, but the bridling process really is just too time consuming."

Basic Kite-Fishing Setup

Kite line (50-pound Dacron)

Wind

Kite rod with electric reel

Dropback Debate

Dropping back is another important consideration in kite fishing. Some anglers prefer letting a fish run with the bait while the line remains in the kite clip (also referred to as a "pin"), while others like to snap the line from the clip and drop back to the fish straight from the fishing rod. "The dropback is a Catch-22, but you really can't go wrong if you let them eat it a while with the line in the pin," Randy says. "If I see a fish come up on the bait, I like to drop it back via the clip. Once the fish has taken the bait it will accelerate. That's when you can lock up and come tight on them."

Towe adds that many people don't fish kites because they feel it's too much trouble. One sure way to make it easier on yourself is to spring for an electric kite reel. "Once you've seen how easy electric reels make it, you'll never wind in another kite by hand," Randy exclaims. "It's an apples-to-oranges difference."

By experimenting with kites you can add a new dimension to your fishing arsenal. Kites can produce on slow days when conventional techniques fail, but perhaps equally important is the excitement factor. Very little in offshore fishing is as exciting as watching a fish crash or skyrocket on a frantic baitfish fluttering on the surface. It's what live-bait fishing is all about, and kites take it to another level. Try it for yourself and see why captains like Randy Towe never leave the dock without a kite aboard.

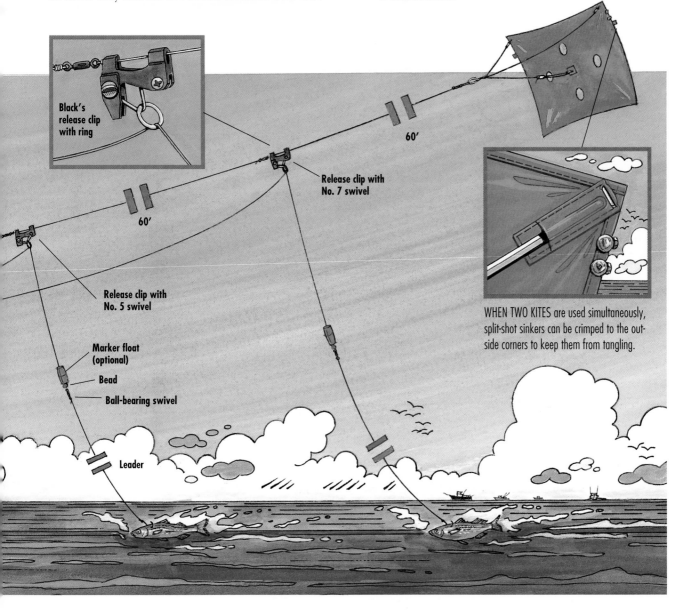

Black's release clip with ring

60'

Release clip with No. 7 swivel

60'

Release clip with No. 5 swivel

Marker float (optional)

Bead

Ball-bearing swivel

Leader

WHEN TWO KITES are used simultaneously, split-shot sinkers can be crimped to the outside corners to keep them from tangling.

OFFSHORE TECHNIQUES:

Coming Full Circle on Billfish

by Scott Boyan

Committed to conservation, Joan Vernon, Ron Hamlin and Tim Choate have redefined billfishing in Central America by using circle hooks.

Blue Marlin

It was in November 1998, during the Presidential Challenge of Central America, when tournament organizer Joan Vernon, along with Captain Ron Hamlin of the *Captain Hook* and Tim Choate of Artmarina, took a major step in helping to conserve Central America's billfish. Of the 421 billfish released during the three-day event, over 100 were caught on circle hooks, a new approach considered to be among the most important developments in the effort to decrease billfish mortality in the recreational sector.

In a landmark decision, Vernon announced at the tournament's conclusion that the Presidential Challenge was abandoning conventional J-hooks for the radical circle hook – permanently – starting in 1999. The decision makes it the first billfish tournament in the world to do so, a change that was apropos considering that the tournament's top angler award went to Choate with 26 sailfish releases – all of which were caught on circle hooks. But even more impressive is the fact that Choate's Fins 'n Feathers Inn in Guatemala has also switched to using circle hooks full-time – the first billfish lodge to do so. Nor will you find any other type of hook on Hamlin's boat – the first charter boat to rig all its baits with circle hooks.

"Someone must take the plunge," exclaimed Vernon. "The Presidential Challenge is committed to billfish conservation, and we will go to great lengths to educate anglers and crews in the effective use of circle hooks."

But what warranted the switch? Too many gut-hooked fish, or was it simply refinement? "We went to circle hooks strictly in a conservation move," says Choate. "We knew that even if the catch ratio was less, the conservation value would overwhelm the loss of caught fish. What we found, however, is that the hook ratios are equal to, and in most cases, better."

In the past, captains and conservationists have complained about the practice of long drop backs with J-hooks, a technique linked to gut-hooking and increased mortality. Yet the circle hook, which tends to catch in the fish's jaw a high percentage of the time, radically reduces that risk. Many believe this method looms as the most important advance for conservation to date. Used on almost every salt water species throughout the world today, circle hooks have already been tested successfully on several species of billfish, including Atlantic and Pacific sailfish, and blue, black, white and striped marlin.

This wasn't the first time that circle hooks have made headlines. In June, '98, Hamlin joined Tim

Choate, Peter Wright and Skip Walton at Fins 'n Feathers to test the concept further. The group originally tried rigging the hooks in the stomachs of ballyhoo, just as they would with J-hooks, but it simply didn't work.

In the end it was Hamlin's original rigging design – bridle-rigging the circle hook to the ballyhoo's head – that proved most successful. In fact, Hamlin has been so successful using circle hooks that in 1998 he was presented the Pacific Sailfish Award from The Billfish Foundation as top release captain. (In Hamlin's case, it happened to be the most billfish ever tagged by anyone in a year's time.) He was also awarded AFTCO's Pacific Captain of the Year and the IGFA's Conservation Award for his efforts in proving the effectiveness of using circle hooks to catch billfish. As if that wasn't enough, in December of 1998 his boat released 145 sailfish in three days, one of which was a single-day release record for sailfish – 71.

Taking the Plunge

"There were two reasons for taking the plunge," Vernon explained. "One was to increase the fish's chances for survival. The second was the fact that anglers during this year's Presidential Challenge were so eager to try an entirely new technique, voluntarily, in a tournament. That astounded me. That's when I said, 'Why not just do it?' So I did. I announced the switch to circle hooks right there."

Used exclusively at Fins 'n Feathers for sailfish, the Eagle Claw L2004 7/0 is also the official hook of the Presidential Challenge. Despite the variety of circle hooks on the market today, the L2004 has several qualities that made it the hook of choice. Slightly offset and featuring mid-wire weight and a black-pearl finish, the carbon steel L2004 is the right size and weight for ballyhoo. And since they're pre-sharpened, they're ready to fish right out of the box. The L2004 is available in tackle shops and most mail-order catalogs.

For larger billfish such as blue marlin, Hamlin and the Fins 'n Feather crews switch to an Eagle Claw 190 16/0 circle hook, although they have caught blue and striped marlin on the L2004 7/0. Their marlin setup is similar to the ballyhoo rig, except they'll use Spanish mackerel and split-tail mullet with more stitching since the marlin bite is more aggressive. In March of 1999, Hamlin and his crew released a 1,000-pound-plus blue marlin on this rig.

Aside from convincing stubborn anglers to try something new, the biggest hurdle may be teaching them how to rig with circle hooks. But as Vernon reminds everyone, there was once a time when we had to learn how to rig ballyhoo with J-hooks too. To help the cause, she and Hamlin held a seminar at the Miami Boat Show in February to teach anglers the proper rigging technique, and in September Hamlin will travel to Venezuela to teach the crews there.

According to an Eagle Claw representative, it's going to take people a while to learn the rigging process. "People are just figuring out how to use circle hooks, so there's still a little resistance because it's so radical, but I think more billfishermen will start experimenting with them. It's like going from a typewriter to a computer. It's an awesome thing, and you have to do things differently, but the end results are a whole lot better."

Just the Facts

Fish hooked in the gills or gut have a dramatically lower survival rate than those hooked in the outer portion of the mouth. Knowing that the type of hook you use can make a difference, billfishermen should seriously consider the facts about circle and J-hooks. At Fins 'n Feathers, before switching over to circle hooks, the boat's average catch ratio with J-hooks was 50 to 56 percent.

In contrast, the results with circle hooks are quite different. According to Hamlin, his boat is now featuring a 66- to 69-percent catch ratio. Is that accurate? "Very accurate. An inexperienced angler who wants to hook his or her own fish is going to catch 50 percent. A good angler who wants to hook his own fish is going to average 70 percent. You let my mates hook the fish and we're going to average 80 percent."

And how many of those are gut-hooked? "The bleeding and gut-hooking is almost zero," says Choate. Knowing that fish hooked in the jaw stand a good chance of survival, it makes sense that anglers consider using circle hooks to protect the resource. But the jaw-hook rate isn't the only benefit of this radical hook. According to Hamlin, one of the most underrated qualities of the circle hook is that billfish will often charge at a bait again and again without ever getting stung by the hook's point. And due to its unique design, once the fish is hooked, it stays hooked.

So, the question begs to be answered: If circle hooks are better for the fish and are just as productive as J-hooks, why aren't more captains experimenting with them? According to the trio, they will be; it's just a matter of time. "The faster we have the highly publicized captains in the business start fishing with circle hooks – the Peter Wrights, the Bobby Browns, the John Baylisses, the Chip Shafers, the Dave Nolings – the faster the rest of the angling public will jump into line," says Hamlin. "The fish jump more, and they fight harder because they're not lethargic from being gut-hooked."

To get a scientific opinion, Dr. Eric Prince from the National Marine Fisheries Service (NMFS) was invited to Fins 'n Feathers in April of 1999 to evaluate the impact both circle and J-hooks have on billfish. The study's goal was to gather clear-cut scientific conclusions that will enable all sport fishermen to have confidence that their release rate really is a "live" release rate.

Currently Hamlin is turning in a record of his daily catches to NMFS, in which he records the condition and hook location of every fish. Similar studies have been done on salmon in California, and the findings were so compelling that the state now requires the use of barbless circle hooks.

"I haven't seen a down-side to this situation at all," says Hamlin, "and it's going to put even more

pressure on billfishermen to consider circle hooks. If they catch in the billfish's mouth a good percentage of the time, why not test them out? Any fish is going to be in far better condition."

And according to Choate, anybody who has caught a sailfish on a J-hook can do it just as easily with a circle hook. In fact, a number of anglers converted to circle hooks during the Presidential Challenge. "I was very impressed with the people that were open-minded enough to do it," reiterated Choate, "but no matter how new those anglers were to circle hooks, they finished with better averages than those using J-hooks!"

Is this a contagious trend? "I certainly hope so," says Vernon. As a matter of fact, 1998 Isla Mujeres Ladies Tournament winner Anthony Mendillo Jr. of the *Keen M* is already testing circle hooks on Atlantic sailfish in Mexico's Isla Mujeres/Cancun area. Also having early success with circle hooks were Captain Bouncer Smith in Miami and sailfish guru Nick Smith in Palm Beach with live bait – a concept that this author first developed with Nick Smith in 1996.

So what does the future hold for this approach? Time will tell. Whether it will ever be accepted is still a matter of considerable debate. Historically, new techniques have met with resistance. Still, many of today's proven techniques were once ridiculed as being foolish themselves.

Rigging with Circle Hooks

According to Captain Ron Hamlin, the only trick to fishing with circle hooks is changing the way the bait is rigged. The method shown is called a Catalina rig, or head rig, and involves sewing the hook to the top of the bait's head with dental floss.

You can use an egg sinker on this rig, but that's strictly a matter of personal preference. Hamlin opts to rig his baits without sinkers, since he wants as little interference as possible. For the same reason, the use of a bubbler or skirt is strictly prohibited. These items reach the fish's jaw hinge before the hook, impeding the hook set.

As for tackle, the L2004 7/0 is an appropriate sailfish hook on 20- and 30-pound gear. Hamlin has caught blue marlin on the L2004 using 30-pound, and states that the hook won't straighten under heavy pressure.

When targeting marlin, he switches to an Eagle Claw 190 16/0

circle hook. This is an appropriate hook on 50-, 80- and 130-pound tackle. The marlin rig is identical to the ballyhoo rig, except that Spanish mackerel and split-tail mullet are used with more stitching to ensure that the bait holds together during a third, fourth or fifth bite.

The hooking technique is nearly identical to the method used with J-hooks. Hold the rod with the tip pointed at the fish when it hits, then apply only enough thumb pressure to prevent a backlash as the fish takes off with the bait. After a three-second dropback and with the rod still pointed in the direction of the fish, engage the drag and wind until the fish begins pulling line off the reel. If the fish isn't hooked, reel until the bait re-surfaces and prepare to free-spool again if the fish reappears.

by Scott Boyan and Al Ristori

Down to the Wire

by George Poveromo

Improve your catch of blue-water game fish by adding a
wire-line outfit to your offshore arsenal.

In this day and age of high-tech fishing, where lighter tackle is often a prerequisite for scoring more, one technique has weathered the changing tides. Although the extra work involved in trolling wire line may not appeal to some, it still ranks as one of the most potent of techniques. And some days it's the only thing that will put the fish in the box.

Once a charter boat mainstay for taking king mackerel, bonito, barracuda and wahoo, (above) the weight of a wire-line outfit eventually swayed fishermen toward other subsurface trolling options, such as downriggers and planers, that promoted the use of lighter tackle. However, wire's ability to catch fish has never waned, and custom wire-line outfits are suddenly resurfacing on both small and large boats whose captains are seeking more strikes from wahoo, king mackerel, and even tuna and dolphin.

The advantages of wire line include its ability to position a bait several feet beneath the surface.

Wire produces throughout the season, yet it really shines when warm surface temperatures keep bait and game fish in the depths. And its compatibility with faster trolling speeds often tempts more wahoo and tuna.

"Wire line catches fish. It's that simple," says Harry Vernon III, the proprietor of Capt. Harry's Fishing Supply in Miami and a wire-line expert. Vernon's experience with trolling wire line spans decades. He not only fishes the stuff for wahoo, kingfish and tuna off South Florida and the Bahamas aboard his 31-foot center console, he also trolls it along the reefs for big grouper.

A Basic Outfit

For general wire-line trolling, Vernon uses a Penn Senator 9/0 reel, "a dependable workhorse." The reel is attached to a custom-built, seven-foot, curved-butt rod equipped with either carbide-ring or

AFTCO Big Foot guides and a swivel tip. The swivel tip, a must for offshore wire-line trolling, follows the angle of the line and prevents it from kinking. Vernon also recommends a Lee's Swivel Rod Holder, which can be adjusted to keep the rod facing outward and away from the other trolling lines. On the strike, the rod swings toward the fish so line can flow straight through the swivel tip.

Vernon favors a curved-butt rod because it places the line closer to the water, enabling the lure to run deeper. This arrangement is also less likely to interfere with the other lines, and allows Vernon to leave the rod in the holder while fighting a fish. Aboard a larger boat, the outfit can be trolled from a fighting-chair gimbal. However, to prevent the rod from being pulled overboard, a pin must be inserted in a hole drilled through the rod butt and the gimbal cup on the chair.

Vernon fills his reel with .035-diameter (125-pound-test) stainless-steel wire, connecting it to the spool with a tight haywire twist. The 9/0 Senator holds approximately six pounds of wire, and there's about 275 feet of wire per pound. Stainless wire is less expensive than Monel wire, although it's much stiffer and more difficult to handle. It's also stronger per diameter. For example, .035 stainless wire is rated at approximately 125-pound test, whereas .035 Monel is rated at 80-pound test. On the other hand, Monel, which contains more nickel, is much softer, easier to work with and less prone to backlashes. Prices vary from about $9.50 per pound for stainless to around $18.50 per pound for Monel. Both materials require a little extra care to maintain. "Stainless rusts and Monel corrodes if neglected," says Vernon. "Always spray lubricant on the wire after each trip, one that leaves a protective coating."

After the reel has been filled, the wire is threaded through a half-ounce egg sinker and attached to an X67CZ Sampo ball-bearing snap swivel with a haywire twist. The purpose of the egg sinker is to keep the swivel from accidentally jamming in the rod tip. A 16-ounce cigar sinker is then clipped to the snap swivel, with the opposite end of the sinker clipped to another snap swivel that has been crimped to one end of a 12-inch, 300-pound-test monofilament shock leader. Another X67CZ snap swivel is crimped onto the opposite end of the monofilament and clipped to 30 feet of No. 10 (131-pound-test) stainless wire leader ending in a 3½ Drone

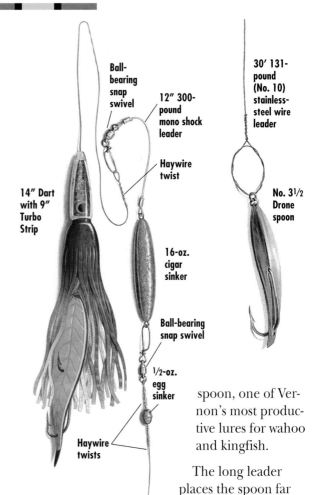

Ball-bearing snap swivel

12" 300-pound mono shock leader

30' 131-pound (No. 10) stainless-steel wire leader

Haywire twist

14" Dart with 9" Turbo Strip

No. 3½ Drone spoon

16-oz. cigar sinker

Ball-bearing snap swivel

½-oz. egg sinker

Haywire twists

spoon, one of Vernon's most productive lures for wahoo and kingfish.

The long leader places the spoon far behind the large cigar sinker and contributes to its erratic, wobbling action. Another advantage of the spoon is that its swimming action is telegraphed through the rod tip. Should the lure snag some weeds, the rod tip will stop pulsating, alerting you to the problem.

While Vernon's trusty Drone spoon accounts for a variety of offshore fish, other effective wire-line lures include the eight- to 12-ounce C&H Feather, the R&S Mini Dart (eight inches) and Tuna Dart (14 inches), the eight- and 16-ounce Capt. Harry's Dart, and the eight-ounce Billy Bait. Unless he plans on high-speed trolling, Vernon pulls these heavier baits on an eight-foot leader with no cigar sinker.

Shocking Technique

The mono shock leader in Vernon's terminal setup prevents shock in two ways. It not only acts as a shock absorber when fighting a fish, it prevents the static charge generated by high-speed trolling from shocking the angler when he grabs the outfit! It also prevents electrolysis from corroding or weakening the wire, terminal components and even the reel spool.

With this setup and a trolling speed of between 8 and 12 knots, Vernon expects the lure to get down ten feet for every 100 feet of line paid out. To mark the wire so he knows how much is being let out, Vernon cuts four thin strips of white or yellow 3M tape and wraps one strip at the 100-foot mark, two strips at the 200-foot mark and one strip at the 300-foot mark. He recommends wrapping the strips toward the rod tip and coating them with Crazy Glue to keep them from unraveling.

Because of the wire's weight and resistance, be sure to let it out slowly when setting the spread. Some anglers simply use the reel's drag to let the line out slowly, while others apply firm thumb pressure to the spool. Letting the line run out unchecked and then throwing the reel into gear can break or damage the pinion gear.

Beating a fish on wire requires an even, steady retrieve. When the fish stops running, straddle or sit on the edge of the gunwale (if you don't have a fighting chair) and begin the task of cranking in line while keeping the rod in its holder. Because some offshore fish have relatively soft mouths, excessive pressure can tear a hole large enough for the hook to slip out. That's why moderate drag settings are recommended. Vernon sets his drags at 10 to 12 pounds, and always keeps the boat moving forward during the fight and the leadering process to maintain a tight line.

Once the angler winds the sinker to the rod tip (a must to prevent an injury), a member of the crew should grab the long leader and begin leading the fish in with a steady, continuous motion. Instead of placing the wire leader in the cockpit where it could wrap around someone's leg and cause a serious injury should the fish charge off, feed it overboard. The forward motion of the boat will keep it away from the vessel and the fish, and prevent it from kinking. Once the fish has been boated or released, the leader can be checked for damage by running it through your hand as the line is being let out.

Although Vernon usually trolls one wire-line outfit among his spread of surface baits, he says it's no problem to troll two of them, as long as sharp turns are avoided. He also points out that it's a good idea to stagger the lure depths to cover different portions of the water column.

Anyone who doubts the effectiveness of wire-line trolling need only join Vernon for a day of offshore trolling or reef fishing. It's sure to be an eye-opening experience. As for the veteran wire-line troller himself, Vernon has this to say: "If you're not using wire, you're missing a lot of fish. In the long run, it'll end up being one of your most dependable trolling outfits."

Wire on Stand-Up

Ray McConnell of Ray's Offshore Tackle in Boca Raton, Florida, specializes in building wire-line outfits for his customers who want to fish them stand-up style. "A wire-line outfit will out-fish other trolling outfits ten to one," says McConnell. "But when you take a wire-line outfit built around a seven- or eight-foot rod and a 9/0 reel, that's a very heavy piece of equipment. I wanted to lighten everything up and put more sport into it."

McConnell's outfits are based on a two-speed Shimano 30-pound-class reel, although he says a Penn 6/0 is a good alternative. He spools on 150 yards of 80-pound monofilament, then uses an Albright knot to connect the monofilament to 600 feet of 80-pound-test stainless wire. "Most of the wahoo we catch around here pose little threat of stripping these reels," says Ray. "However, if you're going to fast-troll for wahoo in the Bahamas, where the fish are bigger, you'll need to lose the mono backing and go with straight wire to gain the extra line capacity."

The reel is attached to a 5½-foot, 40- to 60-pound-class stand-up rod outfitted with hardened roller guides and a swivel tip. "The combination is light and easy to handle with a fish on," says McConnell. "It's also perfect for small-boat fishing, because it doesn't take up much room and is easy to store.

"The short rod and two-speed reel provide the leverage and power to fight a fish. If you have a decent-size fish on the line, drop the reel into low gear. It makes life easier." To prevent the wire from kinking, McConnell talks about developing a rhythm that allows line to be wound smoothly onto the spool.

McConnell's terminal gear consists of a 16- to 32-ounce cigar sinker connected to a 20- to 30-foot, 200- to 300-pound-test mono shock leader via a ball-bearing swivel. He runs at least 12 inches of wire off each side of the cigar sinker to prevent a cut-off should a wahoo or kingfish take a swipe at it. Another ball-bearing swivel is used to attach the shock leader to a 10- to 15-foot wire leader. When it comes to lures, Ray favors the double-skirted, 10-ounce Gulf Stream lure, the California-made Burns Bomber and the eight-ounce, Mylar-skirted Billy Bait Super Magnum.

Five Trolling Tactics that Work!

by George Poveromo

This expert advice will help you increase your offshore trolling success no matter where you fish.

The strike came out of the blue and a big dolphin cart-wheeled into the air some 200 feet behind our boat. Mark Cellura cleared the remaining lines, save for the all-blue Ilander-skirted ballyhoo on the long flat line, which we left to drift along during the fight. Talk about making the right move at the right time!

During the final moments of the dolphin battle the flat-line rod buckled over and we heard the distinctive crackling sound of monofilament racing off the reel. No dolphin here! Cellura grabbed that outfit after we subdued the first fish, and 30 minutes later he landed a 66.75-pound wahoo!

Those not versed in offshore trolling sometimes feel that this facet of the sport is a simple, boring undertaking – just point the boat toward the horizon, toss over a few baits, and kick back until something happens. That may sound like an ideal plan, but it's a gross oversimplification. Successful offshore trolling is very demanding, requiring the utmost concentration, skill and preparation of equipment and baits. Like the scenario mentioned above, little tricks can make a big difference.

There are numerous species-specific techniques geared toward catching your favorite offshore game fish, including live-baiting and chunking, but when it comes to general variety trolling for billfish, tuna, dolphin and wahoo there are certain basics that should be adhered to. Below are five important tips guaranteed to make you a better offshore troller.

Choose the Right Baits and Lures

Before creating your bait spread, consider the species that are currently swimming off your coast and the size of the fish you're apt to encounter. Remember that you're looking for variety, so it's not practical to tow a spread of horse ballyhoo or large lures if small to medium dolphin, tuna, sailfish or white marlin avoid them. A blue marlin will certainly eat a big bait, but it'll happily slurp up a small one as well.

For general trolling, consider mixing both a large and a small offering into a spread of medium-size baits. This way, most of your baits will be sized for "action," but you'll have a small bait for enticing less-aggressive or selective fish, and a large bait to provide more splash and dash in hopes of teasing up a real monster. If a certain size bait or lure is drawing most of the attention, though, alter your spread accordingly.

In addition to fishing an odd-sized bait or two, try alternating your baits' swimming characteristics. When pulling naturals like ballyhoo or mullet, add a few swimming baits to a spread of mostly skippers, or vice versa. With lures, try fishing a weighted conehead style with a spread of blunt-headed designs, or vice versa. Sometimes a seemingly trivial change like this can trigger a response.

I'm a firm believer in matching the coloration of the natural offshore forage. If flying fish abound I'll slide an all-blue skirt over at least one of the ballyhoo in the spread. If small dolphin are numerous, I'll choose a skirt matching their hues. I've enjoyed tremendous success with Tournament Tackle's Ilander and Hand Sea Star lures when paired with natural baits, and am confident that the brilliance and realism they add to the baits really fools fish. I also try to "match the hatch" when pulling straight artificials.

Fine-Tune Your Bait Spread

Although there are specialized patterns that produce better for particular game fish under certain conditions, the foundation of a basic yet productive trolling spread centers on organization and isolation. In nature, fish school for protection, and often the weakest members or those that break stride from the others become a predator's meal. That's why I believe it's important to make the bait spread resemble a school of fish.

Consider my basic trolling spread. I prefer to place my closest flat-line bait right where the prop wash fades into clean water. Next, I'll position the long flat-line bait approximately 25 feet beyond the first bait. My short outrigger bait is set some 30 feet behind the bait on the long flat line, whereas my zone for the far outrigger bait is 20 to 25 feet behind the short outrigger bait. The center 'rigger is fished 60 to 80 feet behind the far outrigger bait. This modified diamond pattern mimics a school of moving baitfish, with enough separation between them to elicit strikes. I avoid running baits side by side.

Providing you have enough rod holders and manpower to handle extra outfits, a trolling spread can be enhanced by including additional baits. All it takes is an extra lanyard and release clip on each outrigger.

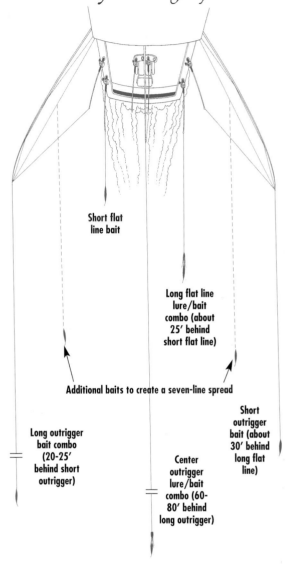

The Author's Favorite Variety Trolling Spread

Short flat line bait

Long flat line lure/bait combo (about 25' behind short flat line)

Additional baits to create a seven-line spread

Long outrigger bait combo (20-25' behind short outrigger)

Center outrigger lure/bait combo (60-80' behind long outrigger)

Short outrigger bait (about 30' behind long flat line)

Adjust Your Speed

Many anglers believe in a magic trolling speed. The fact is, each crew has its own criteria based on sea conditions and the type of baits or lures being towed. As a very general rule, natural baits such as ballyhoo, mackerel, mullet and squid perform best between six and ten knots, while blunt-faced lures work best between 8 and 12 knots. Conehead lures troll best between 10 and 15 knots.

To fine-tune a spread, fluctuate your trolling speed and watch the baits. When I'm pulling a mix of skipping and swimming ballyhoo, including one tipped with an Ilander lure, I want the skipping baits to splash along the surface. If they begin jumping out of the water I'll slow down. If they're splashing only occasionally, I'll pick up the pace. The swimming baits should be doing just that – pulsating along underneath the surface. The Ilander/ballyhoo combinations should track just inches beneath the surface most of the time.

Flat-head or blunt-nose lures should break the surface, gulp air and head back down, spewing a smoky trail of bubbles. As the trail begins to fade, the lure should return to the surface for another shot of air. It's a game of fine tuning that generally requires a speed adjustment every time the baits or lures look a little "off." The exception depends upon the fish. If there are few around, try trolling faster to cover more ground. This is also a good time to pull skirted baits or straight artificials, which can withstand the rigors of faster trolling speeds.

Another trick that will add to your spread's attractiveness is the use of weighted baits and transom release clips when seas are rough. Swimming baits are less prone to being whipped from white-capped seas, plus they're more visible below the surface, as opposed to skipping baits. Transom release clips also keep the baits down in rough water. By attaching the flat lines to these release clips (p. 104, top illustration) you'll reduce their angle of entry into the water. Fishing the baits farther back on the outriggers also helps, since the fishing line will dampen much of the whipping action.

Vary Your Trolling Pattern

As a general rule, game fish favor structure such as the edge of the continental shelf, reefs, banks, canyons and humps, areas where bait tends to concentrate. There's also suspended structure such as weedlines, flotsam, rips, buoys, rigs and water-surface temperature variations. All are potential hot spots, especially if they hold bait.

Rather than troll aimlessly around these structures, get creative. Along reefs, contours or the continental shelf, try a zigzag pattern. For instance, if I'm trolling the 100-fathom (600 feet) curve, I'll run parallel to that zone by working in as shallow as 500 feet and as deep as 800 feet, providing the contours are reasonably close together. Your depthsounder is indispensable; monitor it continuously for bait, game fish and temperature variations.

The time to narrow your fishing window is when you get a strike or when you discover bait concentrations. If a marlin or other sizable fish is hooked in 700 feet of water, for example, consider confining your trolling efforts to the 650- through 750-foot depth zone, possibly even tighter if there's a considerable distance between the two depths. The strategy's similar when working temperature breaks, rips and color changes. Zigzag back and forth along the line and occasionally across it until you find action.

Get the Additional Strike

Plenty of potential fish-catching opportunities are lost on the strike. As in the case of the big wahoo mentioned earlier, try leaving at least one line out during the fight, providing it won't interfere with the hooked fish. Dolphin, wahoo, billfish and tuna rarely travel alone. If you hook a big fish and clear all the remaining lines, you could be missing out on a double- or even a triple-header. It doesn't make a difference if the boat is held stationary during the fight, since the sight of a bait wallowing in the water and the thrashing of a hooked fish is often all it takes to get another one to eat.

One of the worst things to do when a fish takes a bait is to shift the boat into neutral. When we hook up, I prefer to keep the boat heading straight and at the same trolling speed for about 30 seconds. That's usually ample time to remove the stretch from the line and ensure a solid hookset, as well as elicit another strike if a companion fish is back there. I never gun the throttles, since the sudden revving of the engines and the baits charging out of the water could discourage additional strikes.

On a final note, if you miss a fish try free-spooling the lure or "crippled" bait back and then jig it to the surface. Provided that the fish wasn't stung by the hook, the sight of the maimed bait freefalling and then erratically darting about often triggers another strike. That's just one more little trick that's brought a few extra fish to our boat!

Rough-Water Trolling Tactics

by George Poveromo

When the wind honks and seas turn sloppy, use these proven trolling strategies to catch fish while others are heading back to the dock.

Getting the most out of offshore trolling hinges largely on how much time and effort you invest in it. You have to know how to locate the game fish, choose the right baits and lures, create a spread that looks realistic and apply practical trolling patterns through productive water. When everything comes together, catching fish on the troll isn't difficult; however, when conditions are less than ideal, it's the fishermen who know how to modify their trolling tactics accordingly who continue to score. Below are several techniques that can help you catch more fish when the wind is howling and seas are up.

Swimming Baits and Heavy Lures

Compared to skipping baits and relatively light, blunt-nosed trolling lures that chum and smoke in calm seas, properly rigged swimming baits and heavy, streamlined lures often excel in rough seas. That's because they're designed to run anywhere from a few inches to a couple of feet below the surface, making them more visible to fish and less vulnerable to wind and waves. Furthermore, swimming baits perform best at slower speeds, which keep you and your crew more comfortable. Slipping a heavy, streamlined lure such as an Ilander, Billy Bait, trolling feather or weighted octopus skirt in front of a skipping ballyhoo, strip bait or squid also helps them stay in the water, in addition to enhancing their appearance.

Another way to keep a natural bait beneath the surface is to rig a cigar-style trolling sinker between the line and leader. Use the lightest sinker you can and still keep the bait running beneath the surface. Planers and downriggers offer similar advantages.

The same basic principle applies to trolling lures. If you're having trouble keeping your lures in the water without trolling too slowly, try switching to heavier jethead or conehead lures, which run better beneath the surface in rough waters. If these lure styles have a drawback, it's that they're designed to be trolled fairly rapidly. Big boats shouldn't have a problem, but it could be a different story aboard a small to mid-size vessel. In this

case, try deploying a spread of large, deep-diving swimming plugs, such as the Rapala CD-18, Yo-Zuri L-Jack Magnum, MirrOlure 113MR, or some of the "Cairns-style" plugs. These lures swim best between five and eight knots, which minimizes pounding in rough seas. Best of all, game fish blast them!

Fish 'Em Farther Back

As a general rule, baits and lures should be fished farther behind the boat when it's rough to minimize the effect of rolling seas. Baits fished close to the transom will swim erratically or could be yanked out of the water as the boat rides up and down steep waves.

Outrigger-style release clips attached to the transom or reel seats are extremely useful for trolling flat-line baits in rough seas, since they significantly reduce the angle of the line, making it less vulnerable

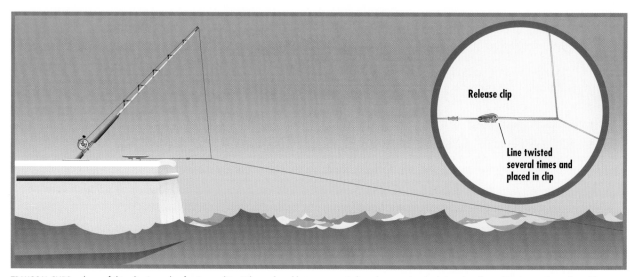

TRANSOM CLIPS reduce a fishing line's angle of entry, making it less vulnerable to strong winds and preventing the bait or lure from skipping on the surface. The use of planers and downriggers will achieve the same thing.

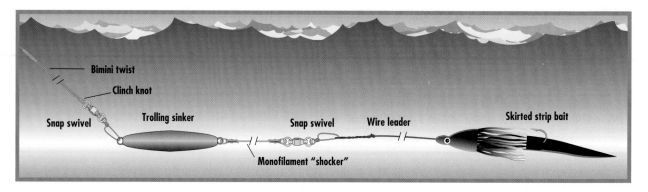

A CIGAR-STYLE TROLLING SINKER placed between the main line and leader is another way to keep baits and lures running below the surface in rough seas. The above is a good setup for wahoo and king mackerel.

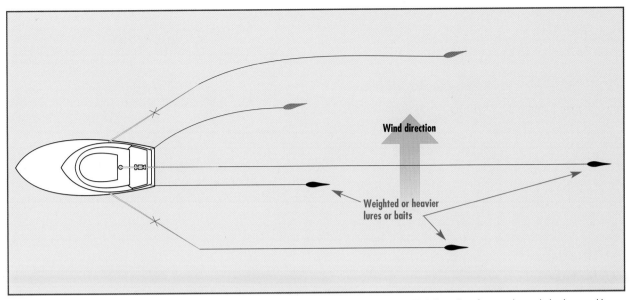

Wind direction

Weighted or heavier
lures or baits

WHEN TROLLING in a quartering or beam sea, running heavy baits or lures on the upwind side of the boat will help keep them from tangling with the downwind lines.

to strong winds and wave tops. Release clips can help in your overall bait positioning, too, allowing you to fish a bait or lure where the prop wash fades to clean water – a hot zone for strikes.

Quartering down-sea produces the smoothest, most efficient trolling course. Avoid trolling directly down-sea, which will produce fluctuating speeds and erratic bait performance. If you want to work along a drop-off, rip, or weedline, position yourself up-sea of the target so that you can troll along it on a quartering down-sea course. In addition to keeping you and your crew reasonably comfortable, your baits and lures will be more visible as they swim down the face of or just beneath the waves.

When you have to turn and troll up-sea, don't head directly into the waves, which will interrupt your trolling speed and the action of the baits. Instead, angle off the seas by around ten degrees, which should dampen the effect of the waves, allowing you to maintain an effective trolling speed.

Trolling at an angle to the wind may require a re-adjustment of the lines to avoid a tangle. For example, if you're trolling toward the south or southeast and the wind is blowing from the east, the port lines may have to be reeled in a bit to keep them from interfering with the starboard lines. This is more critical with the flat lines and center 'rigger line, because of the narrower gap between them. The ideal situation would be for the port flat-line bait or lure to swim ahead of the point where the

starboard flat line enters the water, while the port and starboard outrigger baits, which are positioned well behind the flat lines, should swim ahead of where the center 'rigger line enters the water. This should keep the lines from becoming tangled due to course changes and wind fluctuations. Again, flat-line clips help reduce the trolling angle of the line, further reducing the threat of a tangle.

Turning Tips

To keep the lines apart when changing course, make wide turns. To troll in the opposite direction using the scenario described earlier, begin turning toward the west (down-sea). Gradually come around to the north and begin dropping back the port baits/lures and bringing in the starboard lines to avoid a tangle.

Another tip when faced with gusty breezes is to fish heavier, weighted baits and lures on the upwind side of the spread, since they will hold their positions better while the lighter baits are allowed to drift farther downwind. Of course, it's a lot of work to keep changing baits and their positions, but it's necessary if you want to avoid frustrating and time-consuming tangles.

Trolling in heavy seas isn't exactly a piece of cake. But if the fish are out there and you're willing to brave the elements, try some of these rough-water techniques. They could turn all that rocking and rolling into a successful outing.

The Art of Gaffing

by Capt. Mike "Beak" Hurt

A pro's guide to performing this vital part of the "end game."

More fish are lost at the end of the fight than at any other time. Right when you think you've got 'em you lose 'em. I've seen it happen time after time to potential tournament-winning fish, world records and even just fish that would have been perfect for the barbecue. You probably have plenty of similar stories yourself.

In addition to contributing to lost fish, the end of the fight is also the most dangerous time. Fishermen have been pulled overboard, seriously injured by flying hooks and fish, and worse. However, you can reduce the hazards and losses by using some proven techniques during this end game. Sure, today's anglers are more conservation minded than ever and are learning the correct methods for releasing fish, but if you want to land your catch, you need to be proficient in the art of gaffing.

Choosing a Gaff

The first thing you need to determine is the type of gaff that's best for the job. Just about anything will work – I once used a baseball bat with a piece of bent rebar lashed to it – but there are a variety of gaffs on the market designed for different fish species, sizes and angler preference. Handles and hooks are the basic components, and there are several choices.

Aluminum and fiberglass are the two most popular. Aluminum is rigid and lightweight. Fiberglass handles are usually stronger, tend to be more flexible, but can be heavier than aluminum designs.

The Reliable Gaff Company of Hicksville, New York, offers both aluminum and fiberglass models. According to Manager Bruce Schnur, "Which is 'better' depends on the user." He said he really couldn't recommend one over the other. However, he did explain that there is a difference in quality among the gaffs on the market. "We make ours strong," he says. "The handles don't break and the hooks don't bend."

AFTCO of Irvine, California, a well-known manufacturer of high-quality gaffs and rod components, went a step further and developed a swage-tapered aluminum handle. The idea was to take the basic design and improve on it by tapering the aluminum handle toward the hook end in order to reduce drag in the water and add strength. AFTCO's Taper-Tip gaffs are now found in the cockpits of serious sportfishing boats worldwide.

Bamboo handles are preferred on board Southern California party boats and the long-range fleet. The crews of these multi-passenger vessels gaff thousands of fish during the season, and although bamboo may not be pretty, it's flexible, light, available in any length, resistant to abuse and salt water, and cheap – but short-lived. Calcutta cane is reputably better than other types of bamboo, as the natural nodes, or knuckles, serve as built-in anti-slip grips. Regardless, most crews wrap the upper half of the handles with cord or twine, a good idea for any gaff.

Handle length depends on boat size more than anything else. "Many anglers think that longer is better," comments Greg Stotesbury, AFTCO's manager and an avid fisherman himself. "A five-foot gaff is plenty long for most small boats." Stotesbury feels that a long gaff restricts maneuverability, but concedes that if the cockpit gunwale or bow is high, a longer gaff is preferable.

Overly long gaff handles, however, encourage "digging," the term for trying to stick a fish that is still very deep. Refraction and water resistance makes this an advanced technique, and rushing the process instead of waiting for a clean shot loses more fish. Finally, to conform to IGFA regulations for taking record fish, the overall length of the gaff, including hook, cannot exceed eight feet.

Hook Choices

Most party and charter boat crews feel the same way about gaff hooks as they do the handle – they like what works best for them. High-carbon-steel hooks, such as those offered by Mustad, may not look very pretty – and will rust – but they don't bend. Most gaffs on the market feature stainless steel hooks because they don't rust, but stainless hooks are softer, and some can bend open. Some of the better gaffs out there are made with heat-treated stainless steel, a process that enhances hardness. One of the newer companies in the gaff business that uses this process is Accurate Fishing Products of Los Angeles, which has its roots in the aerospace industry. "We use aerospace-quality materials," says Accurate's Doug Nilsen. "Many grades of stainless steel, such as the popular 316, are non-magnetic in the annealed condition and cannot be hardened by heat treatment."

Heat-treating can harden the 17-4 aircraft-grade stainless Accurate uses. It's expensive, but offers hardness plus a little "spring" for forgiveness. Accurate gaff hooks won't bend like some lower-grade stainless ones will, or break like "over-heated" stainless or the rigid carbon hooks can.

Hook size and shape is also a consideration. For the average fisherman, a two- to three-inch hook is about right. If the hook is too big, small fish can fall off. On the West Coast, special gaffs for small fish are constructed using a commercial "tuna-feather" double hook. It's especially effective for barracuda, and the gaff is so nicknamed.

For sharks and other big game, a four- to six-inch hook or even a flying gaff may be required. If you're after the giants of the sea, a 12- to 14-inch "flyer" with a reinforced hook is required. Reinforcement is important when you get to this size because the hook's momentum is substantially increased, allowing it to bend more easily. Once a gaff loses its original shape it will never be as strong again.

The shape of the hook is important too. Many pros prefer an open-bite style, in which the point parallels the shank or bends out a little like a question mark. This design will grab the fish easier. A closed-bite hook, where the point bends inward toward the shank, holds the fish better, but makes it harder to sink the point. In general, the shorter the shank and point, the better, as chances of the hook bending open are reduced.

There's no need for a barb on most gaffs. A barb may help the novice hold onto the fish more easily after it has been gaffed, but it makes it difficult to get the fish off, and can create a big hole, ruining some good meat. The only time I use a gaff with a barb is for "special" fish that I just plain can't afford to lose. And just like your fishing hook, gaff points should be kept as sharp as possible and checked routinely.

I recommend keeping a variety of gaffs on board. Even if you normally target small fish, you never know when a monster might show up. I've heard more than one story of a crew taking longer to land the fish after it was gaffed than it took the angler to bring the fish to boatside. I like to set up a matching set of gaffs and tag poles on each side of the boat, within easy reach in case I need one in a hurry.

Gaffing Techniques

A lot of fish are lost due to poor gaffing techniques. The first job is to clear the cockpit. Get the hoses, buckets, brushes, lures and other rods out of the area. You don't want anything in your way while fighting, gaffing or landing a fish. Regardless of how tight the area is, keep things organized. A cluttered cockpit can cause problems or injury.

Next, communicate! Crew and angler should talk to each other, especially if they're not used to fishing together. Gaffing is a team effort. Many botched gaff jobs can actually be traced back to the angler not acting in concert with the crew, so both angler and gaffer should be on the same page. Each person has his own responsibilities.

If you're the angler, yell out when you see the fish, or shout "color," and make sure the fish is under control as it comes up. You should always stay directly in front of the fish "no angles, no tangles." You may have to make a few quick moves to keep the fish from going under the boat or tangling with another fish. Never be afraid of dipping your rod tip in the water; if the fish gets under the boat, you need to get the rod down as far as you can so the line will clear the running gear. Once the fish is under control, guide it into position and present it to the gaffer. Never lift the fish's head out of the water, as this can really make it go crazy. And stay at the rail. Don't step backwards in order to bring the fish a few inches closer – stay where you can see what's going on.

If you're the gaffer, after the angler yells "color!"

you should ready the gaff and stand by, keeping the handle out of the way. Hold it alongside you with the hook up. As the fish is presented, you should lead it and take aim behind the line or leader. Gaff the fish with a quick, decisive pull, then bring the fish to the boat and control it.

As soon as the fish is gaffed, the angler should immediately focus his attention on the gaffer while keeping the rod tip pointing up. He should engage the clicker and back off on the drag (or put the reel in free-spool, being careful to prevent a backlash). If the fish somehow gets off the gaff and bolts away, nobody should try to stop it. Be ready for this scenario with offshore fish such as tuna and wahoo. Put the reel back in gear or increase the drag when the fish is clear of any potential problems and has finished its initial burst.

Mate Overboard!

Try not to position the gaff in front of the line. If the fish makes a sudden move you can get into trouble real fast, and if the gaff touches the line you may break the fish off. I've seen the line act as a lever and pop fish off the gaff and fishermen off the boat. This is one reason it's important to back off the drag and take the bend out of the rod so that the gaff alone is taking all the pressure and tension.

Case in point: A few years ago we had a 300-pound swordfish hooked up. During the long battle, I went over all the important end-game duties with the young crew member when to take a shot, where to aim, how to set the gaff hook, why to remove jewelry, the necessity of polarizing sunglasses and gloves, and so on. When the time came and the angler presented the fish, the wide-eyed kid anxiously reached out and, before I could stop him, sank the gaff in the fish. The broadbill blew up, thrashing its huge body while slashing its big sword wildly. Water flew everywhere. I immediately followed up with a second gaff, then a third. When the smoke cleared and the fish was under control, we realized the mate was missing! He had gaffed the fish in front of the leader. When the big sword felt the steel, it bolted, and the leverage of the heavy leader against the gaff handle pulled the young guy right over the side. Luckily, we were able to quickly retrieve him, and the only thing hurt was his pride.

Tips and Tricks

I've seen many fish lost because the gaffer forgot which way the gaff hook was pointing during the initial shot. When I go to stick a fish, I make sure the hook is facing down. I then reach out over the fish and pull the hook into it. In most situations I recommend gaffing over the top of the fish, not under it. You have more control this way and you don't risk tearing the fish's soft belly meat.

To help me know exactly which way the hook is oriented at all times, I developed the habit of holding the gaff handle the same way every time. I automatically know which way the hook is pointing by where my hands are positioned. I guide the gaff with my left hand when the fish approaches, but use my right hand to set the hook. As soon as the hook takes hold, I grab on with my left hand again to help pull the fish close and into the boat.

A head shot is the sign of good gaffing ability and saves meat, but it's an advanced technique that can cost you fish. The best and meatiest place to gaff a fish is in the shoulder. Gaffing in the dorsal area for wigglers like dorado (dolphin), however, makes it easier to control the fish. If you gaff a fish in the tail, you're in for a treat. A "prop-shot" on a big tuna can really shake you up!

Special Fish, Special Techniques

The "personality" or physical characteristics of a fish, and concern for the boat or crew, may call for adaptation in gaffing techniques. Sharks create special hazards because of their jaws, yet with thresher sharks it's the long, slashing tail you have to watch out for. Wahoo and dorado can be tough to control alongside the boat. If the fish has taken a trolled lure and nothing else is going on, I'll keep the boat moving forward at idle speed or even slower. This makes it easier to control and present the fish. Be careful when you swing a dolphin or wahoo aboard; if it gets off the gaff it can make a real mess of the cockpit. And there are plenty of stories about lures being fired from fish mouths, with the hooks going into waiting arms and legs. One remedy is to put a wet towel over the fish, which will often calm it somewhat. A couple of good raps to the forehead with the fish bat is a humane way of dispatching your catch, saves the meat from being bruised, and reduces wear and tear on the boat. Bleed the fish right away and get it on ice or into an insulated fish bag promptly to preserve its quality.

The Pacific halibut is another fish with special characteristics that is very dangerous if not gaffed and handled properly. Tom Ohaus, *SWS*'s Northwest Editor, has fished 'buts for years. "Halibut do not expend their energy during the hookup," he explains. "You should always consider these fish as 'green' when you gaff them, regardless of how subdued they seem."

Because of how dangerous a 100-plus-pound halibut can be in the back of the boat, Ohaus and other guides prefer (for safety's sake) to shoot the fish before pulling it on board. "A single-shot .410 shotgun is best, and aim for the head, behind the eyes," he recommends. Bullets are not as effective, says Ohaus, and are more apt to ricochet off the water. Of course, shooting a fish will disqualify it as an IGFA record – and it can be dangerous – so take heed.

If you don't want to shoot the halibut, Ohaus recommends gaffing the fish in the gut, just behind the gills. Pull it on board, strike it on the head with the bat, and put it in the box in one continuous move. The less time a big halibut spends on deck, the better. A harpoon can be used on a really huge halibut. The dart is placed in the fish's head and the line is looped around the tail and drawn tight. The fish is then "bowed" so it can't flop around.

Many anglers who pursue very large fish use flying gaffs. The hook on a flying gaff is designed to disengage from the handle and is attached to a line that you hold onto (instead of the handle). A flying gaff is preferred for big game such as blue and black marlin, giant tuna, or outsized sharks that can be dangerous or hard to control after being "stuck."

If you don't have a lot of experience using a flying gaff, one of the problems you may encounter is attaching the head (hook) to the handle in such a way that you are able to sink the point into the fish, yet easily break the handle free. Manufacturers have come up with different ways of releasing the head, ranging from a twist-lock mechanical configuration to tying the head to the shaft with a piece of line. With this latter, time-proven method, the handle will have a conduit in the end to accept the hook, and a slot for the rope-attachment ring to prevent the head from twisting. A few wraps of 20-pound line around this ring (or a separate molded-in cleat) and the "rivet" or cleat on the handle will keep the head attached. But be careful, if you use too strong a line you won't be able to break the head free after you've stuck the fish, and an out-of-control flying gaff handle is nothing you want to fool with.

As an alternative, on some gaffs I'll use masking tape to secure the head to the handle. I put about three wraps of tape around the line and handle at the head of the gaff, and several more wraps a few feet up the handle. Don't use electrical or duct tape, as you may have trouble breaking it when you need to.

The end of the gaff line (many gaffs come with 30 feet of rope per IGFA maximum) should be attached to the boat somewhere. Thirty feet is really more than enough, because if a fish gets away from the gaffer it can get enough of a running start to tear free from the gaff hook. Nevertheless, if you attach the end of the line to an aft cleat you'll be able to reach the fish no matter where in the cockpit it's being landed. If you have a fighting chair, the pedestal can serve as the center point for attaching the line. However, I don't like this arrangement, since it leaves line on the deck for someone to turn an ankle on or trip over, and can be downright dangerous when a big marlin or tuna has been stuck. Instead, I like to run a rope (dockline) from one stem cleat, out through the hawsepipe, then along the outside of the transom and back in the hawsepipe on the other side, where I pull it tight and fasten it to the opposite cleat. I then tie a loop knot around this line with the gaff line. I make the gaff line as short as I can and still be able to gaff a fish anywhere I can physically reach from the cockpit. The gaff line usually ends up being significantly shorter than 30 feet, but this setup allows you to travel from one side of the boat to the other while keeping the line out of the way.

When I make a shot with a flyer, I take a wrap on the gaff line with my right hand, pull tight, and take hold of the end of the handle. I guide the gaff with my left hand, and when I stick the fish I hold onto the line with my right hand and remove the handle with my left. Depending on the situation, a second and even third gaff may be necessary. We don't take any chances.

The point of this article is that the end game in a fish-fight is just as important as, if not more important than, the beginning. Whether you're going to land the fish or tag and release it, take this task very seriously. Experience is the best teacher, but you can practice the basics. When I was a "pinhead" on the party boats, I had to prove I could gaff before graduating to deckhand or mate, so I practiced precision gaffing on bobbing oranges in the bay. That really smoothed out my technique!

The Paddy Principle

by Tom Waters

For Southern California offshore anglers, kelp paddies, free-floating on the open ocean, can be the key to finding fish during the summer and fall months.

It's been a couple of summers now, but the skipper's words still ring in my ears: "You should have been out with us yesterday. We killed 'em!"

I winced. Maybe I'm superstitious, but I get real uncomfortable when I hear those "you should have been here yesterday" stories.

"Yeah, we trolled for tuna outside all day with no strikes and then we spotted this kelp paddy," he continued. "Made a half-dozen drifts by it, used up all our bait, and everyone came home with full sacks of yellows and dorado – big fish, too – up to 30 pounds!"

Ouch! You hate to think you missed that kind of fishing by only a few hours, so you head out to sea,

knowing that your skipper will never locate the same drifting kelp paddy, but hoping that he finds another just like it, loaded with the same kind of hungry fish.

Unfortunately, we weren't so lucky on that day, although other boats were. In fact, during the summer and fall months in southern California, there are plenty of anglers – private boaters and party-boaters alike – who cash in on some exciting action under free-floating kelp paddies. After all, this is the time of year when "exotic" pelagic fish – marlin, tunas, yellowtail and dorado – migrate northward from Baja (Mexico) waters, and it is not unusual to find any or all of these game fish schooling beneath canopies of kelp.

Paddy Protection

Most free-floating kelp paddies encountered by Southern California anglers are composed primarily of intertwined stringers of giant kelp (*Macrocystis pyrifera*). What's curious is that giant kelp characteristically grows in 100 feet of water or less in close proximity to the mainland and offshore islands from central California south to central Baja's prominent Point Eugenia. Why then, are larger pieces of this algae – sometimes entire plants – found floating in open-ocean waters and as far south as southern Baja?

have been reaping the ocean's bounty from beneath both natural and man-made floating objects. Native fishermen in the South Pacific are thought to have been the first to deliberately place structures in the open sea to attract concentrations of food fish. Bamboo rafts continue to be favorite fish-attracting devices in the Philippines and Indonesia while tree trunks, palm fronds and various other flotsam have been, and continue to be, used as attractors by fishermen in the Mediterranean, western Australia, the Indian Ocean, Japan and many of

Biologists speculate that strong currents and heavy seas created by severe winter storms that periodically sweep down from the Gulf of Alaska cause tangled masses of the kelp to be torn loose and set adrift. Seemingly most susceptible to such damage would be the large kelp forests growing around southern California's outermost islands: San Miguel (westernmost of the Channel Islands), San Nicholas (about 60 miles offshore) and San Clemente (about 45 miles from the mainland).

Southern California's prevailing offshore winds and south-flowing currents push the floating kelp down the coast. How fast and how far the kelp paddies travel depends on changing weather and water conditions. Some wash up on Southern California beaches, while other float well offshore for who knows how long or how far. What's even more interesting is that the free-floating kelp continues to grow, particularly if the holdfast is still attached, so it's conceivable that the same paddy could be floating about for a couple of years, given the appropriate amount of sunlight, adequate nutrients and tolerable water temperatures.

What's the Attraction?

It never ceases to amaze me how many game fish can be found swimming beneath a small piece of floating kelp, yet it should come as no surprise. After all, for centuries, fishermen around the world

the South Pacific islands. In most instances, these floating fish magnets are moored at sea, and could be considered the forerunners of today's FADs (Fish Aggregating Devices) which are large, stationary buoys that have been used with great success in Hawaiian waters to concentrate schools of tuna.

But what is it that makes floating objects such an attraction for so many fish? Interestingly enough, scientists are not sure. Certainly the size of the object is not a critical factor. As any Southern California angler experienced in "paddy hopping" knows, not all floating kelp hold game fish and sometimes a six-foot-wide paddy will produce a huge catch, while a floating kelp canopy ten times that size will be barren. Plus, there are those times when a series of paddies are found floating in the same vicinity; only one holds fish, and with no visible explanation as to why.

It's always exciting to see game fish like yellowtail and dorado cruising just beneath floating kelp as your boat drifts by, but what is observed most often are smaller fish milling around the vegetation, or schools of shimmering baitfish not far below. Obviously, game fish move in around kelp paddies to feed on these small fish. However, certain studies suggest that food isn't the only attraction.

Some scientists speculate that pelagic fish use the

floating objects as points of orientation in an otherwise featureless ocean. That could explain: (1) why game fish can be active around a kelp paddy, suddenly disappear, then return a short while later; (2) why only one in a series of kelp paddies will produce fish at a time, as the school possibly moves from paddy to paddy; and (3) why game fish are seldom found under kelp paddies close to shore, where there are plenty of other features along the relatively shallow bottom that fish can gather around.

Prospecting for Paddies

Prime time for paddy hopping off the southern California coast is from August through October. That's typically the time when striped marlin, yellowtail, dorado and some combination of tunas – yellowfin, bluefin, bigeye, albacore and skipjack (depending on water temperatures) – have migrated north, and any of them, along with thresher, mako and blue sharks, could be patrolling the paddies. The amount of floating kelp can vary from season to season based on the severity of storms during the previous winter, but even when the paddies are numerous, it can require an extensive search to find them.

Because free-floating kelp close to the mainland is usually barren of game fish, the usual approach is to begin prospecting for paddies at least five miles from shore. On the tuna grounds, most skippers choose to troll colorful jigs while keeping one eye on the fishfinder and another on the horizon for signs of surface activity – feeding fish, diving birds and weeds.

On bright, sunny days, the paddies will look amber brown against the cobalt blue of the ocean, and they're relatively easy to spot at a distance. When the skies are overcast, though, the kelp is difficult to see, even with binoculars. Sometimes aiding the effort to spot paddies on gray days are man-made objects – boxes, foam cups, marker buoys, etc. – that may have become entangled in the vegetation and can be visible from some distance. Also, gulls and other seabirds will sometimes perch on the paddy, betraying its location. In other instances, the only indication of floating kelp will be something as subtle as a slick on the downwind side of the paddy.

Creep Up on Kelp

Once a kelp paddy is spotted, care should be taken on the approach. Some skippers will continue trolling, but give the floating kelp a wide berth as they circle in an attempt to drag the lures in tight to the canopy. Meanwhile, the crew is usually chumming the water with a few live baits and the skipper is watching the sonar for signs of fish schooling out away from the paddy or down deep. With this approach, it's not unusual for fish like yellowtail and dorado, the two offshore game fish species most commonly associated with floating kelp, to charge out from beneath the vegetation, boiling on the chum and slamming the lures. Feathered or skirted jigs will usually take dorado, and large mackerel patterned Rapalas are a good bet for the yellowtail.

If trolling fails to produce, the next step is to motor well upwind from the kelp and establish a drift pattern. The idea is to position the boat with the wind on its beam and the stern facing in the direction of the paddy. You don't want to drift into or over the canopy; instead, plan your approach so that you can reach the edge of the vegetation with lob casts and more live-bait chum.

Where large kelp paddies are encountered (some may cover as much as a half acre), private boaters sometimes choose to tie up to the vegetation. The approach of the boat may temporarily spook the fish below, but once the engines are shut down, the boat's hull tends to become nothing more than an extension of the canopy. Given favorable weather conditions, this can be an interesting way to spend the night out on the ocean. A floodlight over the side just might attract smaller baitfish and behind, of course, will be the larger predators. By early morning, you could be locked into some serious fishing action.

Work the Water Column

If the first drift or two by a kelp paddy does not produce any action, don't give up. Game fish can often be in the area, but at the approach of the boat may have scattered or sounded into deeper water for a short period of time. The next move would be to motor farther upwind from the floating kelp, set up the same drift pattern, and begin chumming with chunks of mackerel. This will sometimes serve to draw tuna or yellowtail to the surface. The proper way to do this is to serve up the chum sparingly. Don't drop more than two or three chunks of bait over the side per minute. The baits will drift down slowly, so the process might need to be repeated several times before it produces any results. In these situations, patience can sometimes pay big dividends.

Meanwhile, during each drift, keep busy by pitching metal jigs (UFO, Salas and Sea Strike are popular brands) off the stern, aiming your casts and free-spooling line so that by the time you swing by the paddy you'll be jigging down as deep as 100 feet. Using teamwork, with each angler jigging at different depths, you can speed up the process of locating fish. Yo-yoing the jig as you gradually retrieve it is a proven approach, although yellowtail sometimes respond best to high-speed retrieves through the depths. Blue-and-white, blue-and-chrome, green-and-yellow and "scrambled egg" are productive jig colors.

Whether swimming live baits or casting lures around paddies, keep in mind that the stringers and stalks could be dragging below, perhaps 50 feet deep or so if the holdfasts are still attached. This can be a hazard for bait and lure rigs, and potentially disastrous once you've hooked up.

Typically, most game fish caught around offshore paddies, including tunas and dorado, will run away from the kelp when they feel the sting of the hook; however, yellowtail, the one species most often found under these floating mats of vegetation, will invariably make a run for the weeds, the same way they react when hooked along the coastal kelp beds. That's why it's advisable to use nothing lighter than 20-pound line and a rod with the backbone to turn a yellowtail before it burrows into the floating kelp. Should you fail in the latter, you can always move in and tear up the canopy to get to your catch, but you risk spooking other game fish that might be swimming below – and putting a quick end to what otherwise might have been a great day of fishing.

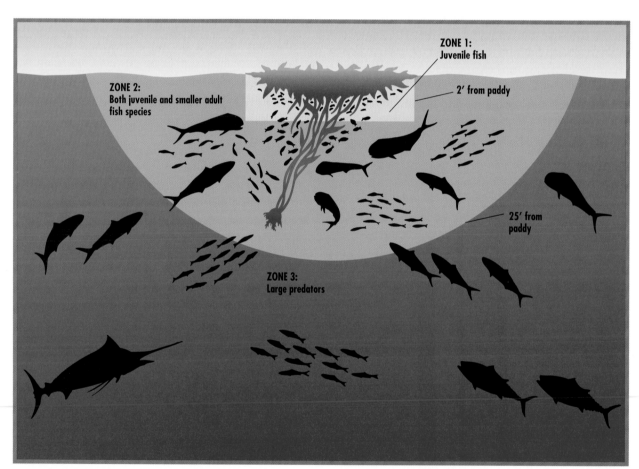

A study conducted in the early 70's showed that the areas around floating kelp paddies can be separated into three distinct zones. Similar zones set up under flotsam in waters around the world.

ZONE 1 Consists of juvenile fish that are under an inch in size and hold tight to the canopy at all times. They do this for protection from predators.

ZONE 2 Ranges from 2 to 25 feet away from the paddy and consists of juvenile and adult fish. These fish swim for the protection of the paddy when larger predators are present.

ZONE 3 Consists of larger predators and can extend out to several hundred feet away from the paddy. Marlin, larger mahimahi, tuna and shark species are common in this zone.

The Teaser Revolution

by Capt. Mike "Beak" Hurt

Innovative fishermen and tackle designers are breaking new ground in their quest for the ultimate offshore fish attractor.

I am always surprised by how many fishermen think teasers are too much of a hassle, a waste of time, or that they scare the fish. If that was the case, why have teasers been around for so long, and why have they been a part of so many noteworthy catches? In fact, anglers and manufacturers continue to experiment with new designs and concepts all the time; especially in recent years. The growing popularity of the bait-and-switch technique has created a surge of interest in surface teasers, and offshore fly fishermen have come to rely on teasers to raise their quarry and lure them within casting range. And, the advent of new materials and rigging techniques has allowed teasers to become more lifelike and effective than ever before. Let's take a look at some of the cutting-edge creations in offshore teasers and how they're being fished.

Changes in the Chain Gang

Daisy chains and spreader bars have been mainstays of the offshore crowd for years. Bluefin tuna fishermen in the Northeast were using these multi-bait attractors long before the rest of the country had even heard about them. Over the years, innovative anglers and tackle companies have taken the basic concept behind the design and expanded it to attract a wider range of game fish.

One new product that reflects this trend is Sevenstrand's Jumping Daisy Chain. "I noticed an increased demand for our small soft lures," explained Sales Manager Bill Goodman, who grew curious about the unusual number of orders he was receiving during a usually slow time of year. "Four of the same color and size were being ordered by some of the better fishermen in our area."

Sevenstrand's Jumping Daisy Chain

Instead of rigging the lures in-line on the same length of mono, like a regular daisy chain, these anglers were crimping them on forward-facing droppers connected to a main section of mono. This caused the little lures to spring forward as they were being pulled through the water, making them seem more lifelike. Goodman eventually began working with some of the fishermen to come up with a better lure to serve the purpose. Sevenstrand even began making its own pre-tied rigs, and offers them with SofTop and Psychosquid lures in a variety of vibrant colors. Similar rigs are being manufactured by a number of companies, among them Mold Craft, Rite Angler and Pacific International Blue Water.

Captain Randy Woods, one of the top billfishermen on the West Coast and the president of Offshore Bait Systems, used to be of the old school when it came to lures. After all, he had been successful with the basics, so why mess with a good thing? However, last year, while fishing on John Crean's *Bounder*, he became a believer in this "new" teaser system. While fishing the Balboa Angling Club's Master Angler billfish tournament, the team deployed the chains from both outriggers, without placing a hook in the last lure. The idea was to attract the attention of a marlin with the chains, then feed the fish a bait on 12- and 16-pound tackle.

"I couldn't believe how long the fish stayed with the chain," Woods told me after the tournament. "Instead of rushing to get one bait in the water, we had plenty of time to rig multiple lines and drop them back. One time we even had a quadruple hookup!" Thanks in large part to the daisy-chain teasers, the *Bounder* crew took second place in the tournament.

Super Spreaders

The spreader bar is another type of multi-lure teaser that has undergone numerous modifications over the years, and there are a variety of materials, sizes and designs now offered. Pacific/International Blue Water, a company that was instrumental in promoting the benefits of daisy chains and spreaders on the West Coast, has come up with what it believes is a better bar material. Made of a plastic composite, it has a number of advantages over the traditional steel bars, according to company president Fred Archer.

"The lightweight bars and the material they're made of help give the rigs lift," Archer says, adding that the lures should splash and dart around like an excited school of baitfish being chased by a predator. He says that the bar should never dive underwater, which reduces the splashing action of the baits. Archer recommends positioning the bar on the face of the wake, with the baits working on the top of the wake and the chase bait trailing on the backside of the wake. Another advantage of the new bars is their flexibility. " This is important when fighting a big fish," Archer says. "A metal bar can bend and even break when a big tuna streaks off with it or a marlin goes ballistic." The new rigs also can be run at higher speeds, which is important when scouting a broad area. Blue Water associate Rick Apple confided that the company has just finished testing a brand new bar. It's made of a thicker material ($7/16$"), measures 40 inches long, and is rigged with 12- and 16-inch squids. According to Apple, the giant bar has taken fish at trolling speeds up to 12 knots.

Deep Dredging

After seeing how well the Fish Trap swimmers worked on offshore fish, I began to look into a new device known as the "dredge," available from Rite Angler. The dredge is basically a heavy-duty version of an umbrella rig, the weighted crossbar spreader so familiar to Northeast striped bass and bluefish anglers. However, instead of sporting a collection of small, plastic tubes, the dredge is rigged with large, soft-plastic baitfish.

When asked to fish Marina El Cid's Billfish Tournament in Mazatlan last season, I called one of my East Coast associates, Captain Skip Smith, to see what he thought of the dredge's potential for taking sailfish. "It's the latest secret for sails in Florida and Mexico," he assured me, adding that the local tournament winners were crushing the fish with it. Smith also noted that the sailfish gang was running them off the outriggers at four to five knots.

Although the rig features a heavy weight in the center of the crossbars, he recommends adding a 32-ounce cigar sinker to the leader about one to two feet in front of it to keep it deep. The dredge is used strictly as a teaser for bait-and-switch. When a fish shows interest, the idea is to drop back a natural bait just inside of the fake bait school – the old "odd-man-out" trick again. Live or dead baits can be substituted for the plastic tails, and Calcutta Bait Co. has recently introduced a lifelike soft ballyhoo imitation called the Bullyhoo that should work well when rigged on the dredge.

Swimbaits for Tuna

Barry Brightenburg of Fish Trap Lures in San Diego makes some of the best soft-plastic swimbaits on the market. He's another manufacturer who noticed an unusual surge in orders during the off-season, and wondered what the lures were being used for.

"Fishermen were ordering boxes of tails in one specific color – Channel Island Anchovy," he recalls. He came to find out that these "inshore" lures were being trolled for albacore and other tunas.

I found out about them when they became the "secret weapon" for small bluefins. Many anglers trolled them on daisy chains and spreaders, but they also worked well as a dropback bait. Following a jig strike, the lure is cast in the wake and free-spooled for 20 or 30 seconds. The lure often gets bit as it sinks.

Last season, I tried trolling these super-supple impostors. I fished one down the middle behind everything else in the spread, and discovered that it worked when nothing else was producing. "That's when they work best," Brightenburg confides. He recommends the five-inch tail with a $1\frac{1}{2}$-ounce shad or tri-head weight for a straighter-running bait. (Tip: place a dab of Super Glue on the hook shank to help hold the tail in position.)

Brightenburg made some small spreader bars with his tails last season, and they proved to be real fish-killers. They even worked on the 50- to

100-pound bigeye tuna that hung around for a while off San Diego, when everyone else was catching only small yellowfins. I've seen similar rigs made with Kalin Dorky Shads, another type of soft-plastic swimbait.

Single Teaser Developments

There have been some new developments in subsurface teasers in recent years, and today you'll find a wide variety of designs – everything from "bowling pins" to mirrored flashers – made by a multitude of manufacturers.

The *Keeper*, a boat out of Catalina Island's Avalon Harbor, did well in the Church Mouse Tournament in the past using one of Braid's Lightning Bolts, a deep-diving, mirrored swimmer. Owner/operator Martin Curtain trolled at seven knots, and ran his two flat lines on the second wake. This put them within ten feet of the teaser, which flashed in the depths like a strobe light.

One of the brightest new stars in the world of big game teasers is the Fish-Fender, which is made by the constantly innovative Mold Craft Co. When I first saw it in George Poveromo's article in *SWS* (see "Marlin on My Fender," February 1998) I got a chuckle, but since then I've heard about how they've become the hot ticket for billfish. One captain even adds a couple of soft-plastic baitfish or squids to the leader on droppers to create a subsurface daisy chain.

Back in the 60s and 70s, we used wide-lipped, angle-nosed swimmers as teasers to help raise fish. One of the most popular was the old Knuckle-Head lure. This jointed lure dove very deep and darted back and forth. It was deployed while slow-trolling dead flying fish off the 'riggers. As high-speed search missions became more popular for finding fish, the chaotic action made them "jumping jigs" – they had a hard time staying in the water, and the fish had an even harder time catching them. Now, with bait-and-switch methods proving so effective, their swimming action is back in demand, and anglers have come up with some tricks for dealing with high trolling speeds.

For instance, if your subsurface teaser isn't performing well at high speeds, try placing it on the back side of the wake. Another trick is to rig a bird in front of the teaser to help hold the lure down. I like to run at least one bird in my pattern anyway; especially for billfish, however, rough weather can be a problem. Ballyhood International makes a bird that works in all conditions. If it gets "sucked down" below the wake, it will come to the surface before popping the outrigger clip. The Ballyhood bird was originally designed to be rigged over a dead bait, but anglers soon discovered that it made a great in-line teaser when rigged ahead of a lure.

Some manufactures have come up with alternatives that wiggle without catching air. EatMe Lures by Aqua Images has introduced a large, concave, pusher-type teaser dubbed Big Eddie. Anglers started rigging them with hooks and they fast became one of the big tournament winners for blue marlin in Baja. The thing that makes this bait special are the two holes in the head. The center hole is best in rough seas, while the upper hole gives the lure a more radical action – good in calm waters when the fish are deeper and are drawn to more movement. In addition to the double action head, the skirts can be changed by unscrewing them from the head.

Mold Craft has addressed the action issue with its new Bobby Brown Special. The added action is achieved by incorporating a weight in the large, angled head. As the teaser swims, the weight travels inside the hollow rubber head to add more wiggle. Keep in mind that this action can also cause more tangles, especially on sharp turns. Also, it's not a good idea to fish two Bobby Browns on the same wake.

Salt Water Sportsman's Top 20 Blue Marlin Hot Spots

Few fish are more highly coveted than blue marlin. Their size, power and noble appearance have led many to consider them the ultimate big-game prize, which is why fishermen will pay big bucks and travel great distances to catch them. if you've always wanted to catch blue marlin, here are 20 destinations (listed in alphabetical order) that will give you a good shot.

Azores

Peak Season: July – October

The Azores are famous for huge marlin. Several fish over 1,000 pounds have been caught by the relatively small charter fleet operating out of Faial. In 1995, over 200 blue marlin, including 12 granders, were caught by just three boats. Definitely a big-fish destination.

Bahamas

Peak Season: March – May

Look to Walkers Cay, Chub Cay, Bimini, and Treasure Cay/Marsh Harbour for the hottest blue marlin action. The fishing peaks from March to May before tapering off in June and July; however, blues can be caught at any time during the year. For large quantities of smaller fish, The Pocket off Chub is best, while smaller quantities of bigger blue can generally be found off Walkers, Bimini, and the Elbow off Abaco's Treasure Cay/Marsh Harbour area. Large fish aren't common, yet a 1,030-pound blue was taken this past May during the third leg of the Bahamas Billfish Championship at Treasure Cay.

Bermuda

Peak Season: June – August

Most of Bermuda's marlin are caught over two deep offshore banks, and the potential for hooking a large fish is good. Many granders have been caught here, including a 1,352-pounder. A few seasons ago, one boat caught 34 marlin in 30 days and another released seven blues in a single day. The season generally starts in May and runs into September, with the peak month being August. Although not a hard-and-fast rule, the larger blues tend to arrive first, followed by smaller fish.

Brazil

Peak Season: October – February

A relatively "new" marlin destination, Brazil has produced some outstanding catches in the last few years, including the current all-tackle world record blue marlin of 1,402 pounds back in 1992. Peak action takes place in the north early in the season and gradually shifts to the south. This is one area to keep an eye on as charter services expand at Rio de Janeiro, Victoria and Comandatuba Island.

Cayman Islands

Peak Season: May – June

Blues tend to run on the small side off the Caymans, but can be plentiful at times. Wahoo, dolphin and tuna are also found here. Peak month is usually June, and boats don't have to travel far to reach deep, blue water. A hot spot for light-tackle and fly gear.

Costa Rica

Peak Season: May – July

Peak action shifts to different parts of the coast depending on time of year. From Guanamar to Tamarindo, prime time is January to March. From Tamarindo north to the Papagayo region, August through December is best. Off Golfito in the south, the fall months are usually prime. Costa Rica offers grand-slam potential, since sailfish, black marlin and striped marlin can be found in the same waters.

Ecuador

Peak Season: December – March

The blue marlin fishery off Manta, Ecuador, can vary greatly from year to year depending on the location of the Humboldt and Equatorial currents. During the last few years, the best fishing has occurred from December to early March, with small blues (up to 300 pounds) arriving first followed by larger fish. The men's 80-pound-line class world record for Pacific blue marlin, a fish of 1,014 pounds, was caught off Manta.

Hawaii

Peak Season: June – September

While summer through early fall is generally considered peak season, blue marlin are always available off Hawaii, and granders have been caught in almost every month of the year. The list of huge blues taken off Hawaii includes a 1,805-pound fish taken in 1971, the largest marlin ever caught on a rod and reel. Hawaii also produced the current all-tackle world-record Pacific blue marlin of 1,376 pounds. Trolling generally begins within a mile of shore, due to the close proximity of deep water.

Jamaica

Peak Season: June – October

Good fishing can be found off Negril, Ocho Rios, and Port Antonio. Larger fish (300 to 400 pounds) show early in the season, with lots of smaller male fish (100 to 300 pounds) arriving in the fall. Port Antonio can be especially productive in October, offering multiple shots each day and making it a great light-tackle marlin destination.

Los Cabos, Baja, Mexico

Peak Season: June – November

Both blue and black marlin are available off the tip of Baja, including some big ones. Last season a blue in the 1,100-pound range was landed off the East Cape. Prime fishing runs through the summer and fall, with the average fish running 250 to 400 pounds.

Madeira

Peak Season: July – October

Madeira has emerged in the last few years as one of the best places in the world to catch blue marlin over 1,000 pounds. Lots of huge fish have been caught here each season, including one estimated at over 1,400 pounds. Trolling usually takes place within 10 miles of shore.

Mauritius

Peak Season: December – March

Located 500 miles east of Madagascar in the Indian

Ocean, the island of Mauritius is another bona fide hot spot for giant blue marlin. More than 20 fish over 1,000 pounds have been taken in the deep waters that lie close to shore, including a 1,430-pounder in 1984 and a 1,355-pounder in 1988.

Mazatlan, Mexico

Peak Season: June – October

Summer brings blue marlin to the waters off Mazatlan, where prime conditions can be found 10 to 20 miles offshore. Small blues come early in the season, with larger fish available later. Average size is 250 to 400 pounds. Many hookups occur while anglers are trolling for yellowfin and dorado, which are also common at this time.

North Carolina

Peak Season: May – September

Although 1996 was somewhat of a bust for blue marlin off North Carolina's Outer Banks due to the effects of Hurricane Bertha, which scattered the sargasso weed along with the dolphin and other bait species, this area historically hosts some excellent action during the summer. The season normally gets rolling in May, with the majority of fish in the 250- to 350-pound class, and peaks during the full-moon period in August. These later fish can run much larger, as typified by a 965-pound brute taken on a charter boat out of Pirate's Cove in Manteo in August, 1995. White marlin action generally takes over by September, but the occasional blue is brought in through October.

Panama

Peak Season: March – May

Panama is most famous for its run of black marlin, but blues are also caught here in good numbers in the spring. Marlin fishing takes place on the famed Hannibal Bank, as well as along the drop-off south of Coiba Island. Fish generally range from 250 to 450 pounds.

Puerto Rico

Peak Season: June – October

When it comes to marlin action off Puerto Rico, the island has a split personality; if you want to catch large numbers of marlin and size is not the main objective, then the southwest part of the island is the best. The action starts to build in late August and builds through October. The majority of the fish are in the 125- to 250-pound range, but the action can be red hot – definitely one of the great areas for light tackle. For those interested in big fish, the north coast near San Juan offers the best potential. The season is June through October, with the best month for big fish being August.

St. Thomas

Peak Season: June – October

Blue marlin fishing off St. Thomas is concentrated primarily along the famous North Drop, a section of the Virgin Bank that gave up the former all-tackle world-record Atlantic blue of 1,282 pounds back in 1977. The mid-90s saw incredible action along the North Drop, with some boats tallying more than 100 fish. In general, bigger (300 to 700 pounds) but fewer blues are caught during the early part of the season, with lots of smaller fish (100 to 300 pounds) providing fast action in September and October.

Turks & Caicos

Peak Season: June – September

Although they lack the notoriety of many bluewater hot spots, the Turks and Caicos offer consistent marlin action from June through September. Located some 500 miles southeast of Florida, these waters offer a mix of small and large fish just 20 minutes from the dock.

Venezuela

Peak Season: March – May

While the peak season for blue marlin off La Guaria, Venezuela, usually occurs in early spring, the fish are always available. For example, the fall occasionally shows good runs of blues, despite the fact that the fall is supposed to be the peak time for white marlin. Five or six blues a day during the spring run is common.

Yucatan, Mexico

Peak Season: April – July

Good numbers of small (200 pound average) blue marlin gather between Cozumel and Cancun during the spring and summer, adding to the fantastic white marlin and sailfish action. A good place to try for an Atlantic billfish slam or for light tackle billfishing.

THE TRAVELING

Atlantic Blue Marlin

Atlantic Blue Marlin: *Makaira nigricans*

Common Names: Blue Marlin, Great Blue Marlin

World Record: 1,402 lbs. 2 oz. – Brazil

Distribution: Azores, Bahamas, Brazil, all Caribbean Islands, Costa Rica, Southeastern U.S.A., Mexico, Western Africa

	January	February	March	April	May	June	July	August	September	October	November	December
1st Choice	Brazil	Venezuela	Venezuela	Venezuela	Virgin Islands	St. Thomas	St. Thomas	St. Thomas	St. Thomas	St. Thomas	Brazil	Brazil
2nd Choice	Venezuela	Brazil	Brazil	Brazil	Venezuela	Ecuador	Madeira	Azores	Madeira	Madeira	Venezuela	Venezuela
Other							Azores		Azores	Puerto Rico		

Pacific Blue Marlin

Pacific Blue Marlin: *Makaira mazara*

Common Names: Blue Marlin, Great Blue Marlin

World Record: 1,376 lbs. – Hawaii

Distribution: Australia, Costa Rica, Ecuador, Hawaii, Panama, South Pacific Islands

	January	February	March	April	May	June	July	August	September	October	November	December
1st Choice	Tahiti, Bora Bora	Tahiti, Bora Bora	Mauritius	Mauritius	Hawaii	Hawaii	Hawaii	Hawaii	Mexico	Mexico	Costa Rica	Tahiti, Bora Bora
2nd Choice	Mauritius		Costa Rica	Hawaii		Ecuador	Mexico	Mexico	Hawaii	Hawaii	Mauritius	Hawaii
Other										Ecuador	Mexico	

Black Marlin

Black Marlin: *Makaira indica*

Common Names: Pacific Black Marlin, Silver Marlin

World Record: 1,560 lbs. – Peru

Distribution: Australia, Costa Rica, East Africa, Ecuador, Mexico, New Zealand, Panama, Peru, South Pacific Islands

	January	February	March	April	May	June	July	August	September	October	November	December
1st Choice	Panama	Panama	Mauritius	Panama	Hawaii	Hawaii	Hawaii	Australia	Australia	Australia	Australia	Panama
2nd Choice	Australia	Mauritius	Panama			Panama	Mexico	Mexico	Mexico	Mexico	Panama	Australia
Other		Australia				Mexico				Ecuador	Mauritius	

White Marlin

White Marlin: *Tetrapturus albidus*

Common Names: Atlantic White Marlin, Spikefish

World Record: 181 lbs. – Peru

Distribution: Bahamas, Brazil, all Caribbean Islands, Costa Rica, East Coast U.S.A., Gulf of Mexico, Venezuela

	January	February	March	April	May	June	July	August	September	October	November	December
1st Choice	Brazil	Brazil	Brazil	Mexico	Mexico	Mexico	Maryland	Venezuela	Venezuela	Venezuela	Brazil	Brazil
2nd Choice	Venezuela	Venezuela	Venezuela	Venezuela	Bahamas	Venezuela	N.Carolina	N.Carolina	N.Carolina	N.Carolina	Venezuela	Venezuela
Other							Venezuela					

Striped Marlin

Striped Marlin: *Tetrapturus audax*

Common Names: Striper, Barred Marlin

World Record: 494 lbs. – New Zealand

Distribution: Australia, California, Chile, Costa Rica, Hawaii, Mexico, South Pacific and Indian Ocean Islands

	January	February	March	April	May	June	July	August	September	October	November	December
1st Choice	Hawaii	Hawaii	New Zealand	Hawaii	Hawaii	Mexico	Maryland	Venezuela	Venezuela	Venezuela	Hawaii	Hawaii
2nd Choice	New Zealand	New Zealand	Mexico	Mexico	Mexico	So. California		So. California	Ecuador	Ecuador	Mexico	New Zealand
Other												

Swordfish

Swordfish: *Xiphias gladius*

Common Names: Broadbill Swordfish, Broadbill

World Record: 1,182 lbs. – Chile

Distribution: Australia, Chile, Ecuador, Mexico, New Zealand, Panama, Peru, South Florida

	January	February	March	April	May	June	July	August	September	October	November	December
1st Choice	Mexico	Mexico	Mexico	Mexico	Venezuela	Venezuela	Venezuela	Venezuela	Mexico	Mexico	Mexico	Mexico
2nd Choice					Mexico	Mexico						
Other												

Pacific Sailfish

Pacific Sailfish: *Istiophorus platypterus*

Common Names: Sailfish

World Record: 221 lbs. – Ecuador

Distribution: Australia, Costa Rica, East Africa, Guatemala, Mexico, Panama, South Pacific and Indian Ocean Islands

	January	February	March	April	May	June	July	August	September	October	November	December
1st Choice	Guatemala	Guatemala	Guatemala	Guatemala	Guatemala	Panama	Mexico	Guatemala	Guatemala	Guatemala	Guatemala	Guatemala
2nd Choice	Costa Rica	Costa Rica	Costa Rica	Costa Rica	Costa Rica	Guatemala	Guatemala	Costa Rica	Costa Rica	Costa Rica	Costa Rica	Costa Rica
Other				Panama		Costa Rica	Costa Rica	Mexico				

Atlantic Sailfish

Atlantic Sailfish: *Istiophorus albicans*

Common Names: Sailfish

World Record: 141 lbs. 1 oz. – Angola

Distribution: Brazil, Florida, Gulf of Mexico, North Carolina, Venezuela, West Coast Africa

	January	February	March	April	May	June	July	August	September	October	November	December
1st Choice	Florida	Florida	Florida	Mexico	Mexico	Mexico	N. Carolina	Venezuela	Venezuela	Venezuela	Florida	Florida
2nd Choice	Venezuela	Brazil		Florida		Venezuela	Florida	Florida	Florida	Florida	Venezuela	Venezuela
Other	Brazil						Venezuela					

Yellowfin Tuna

Yellowfin Tuna: *Thunnus albacares*

Common Names: Ahi, Yellowfin

World Record: 388 lbs. – Mexico

Distribution: Africa, Australia, Bermuda, all Caribbean Islands, Costa Rica, Hawaii, Mexico, New Zealand, all Pacific Islands

	January	February	March	April	May	June	July	August	September	October	November	December
1st Choice	Mexico	Mexico	California (long range)	Mexico	Mexico	Hawaii	Hawaii	Hawaii	Hawaii	Mexico	Mexico	Mexico
2nd Choice			Costa Rica	Bermuda	Hawaii	Mexico	Bermuda	Mexico	Bermuda	So. California		
Other							Mexico		Mexico			

Bluefin Tuna

Bluefin Tuna: *Thunnus thynnus*

Common Names: Horse Mackerel, Southern Bluefin Tuna

World Record: 1,496 lbs. – Nova Scotia, Canada

Distribution: Bahamas, Northeastern U.S.A., Eastern Canada, Southern California

	January	February	March	April	May	June	July	August	September	October	November	December
1st Choice	N. Carolina	N. Carolina	N. Carolina	N. Carolina	New England	Northeast U.S.A.	New England	New England	New England	New England	N. Carolina	N. Carolina
2nd Choice							Eastern Canada	Eastern Canada	Eastern Canada	Eastern Canada		
Other												

Wahoo

Wahoo: *Acanthocybium solandri*

Common Names: 'Hoo, Oahu

World Record: 158 lbs. 8 oz. – Baja, Mexico

Distribution: Bahamas, all Caribbean Islands, Costa Rica, Florida, Hawaii, Mexico, Panama, All Pacific Islands, Western Australia

	January	February	March	April	May	June	July	August	September	October	November	December
1st Choice	Virgin Islands	Virgin Islands	Virgin Islands	Bermuda	Bermuda	Bermuda	Bermuda	Bermuda	Bermuda	Virgin Islands	Virgin Islands	Virgin Islands
2nd Choice	Bahamas	Cayman Islands	Bahamas	Bahamas	Mexico	California (long range)	Hawaii	Hawaii	Virgin Islands	Bahamas	Bahamas	Bahamas
Other							Mexico			Mexico	Mexico	

Dolphin

Dolphin: *Coryphaena hippurus*

Common Names: Mahimahi, Dorado, Dolphinfish

World Record: 88 lbs. – Bahamas

Distribution: Worldwide near all tropical current areas

	January	February	March	April	May	June	July	August	September	October	November	December
1st Choice	Panama	Panama	Puerto Rico	Bahamas	Florida Keys	Florida Keys	Cabo San Lucas	Cape Hatteras	Costa Rica	Guatemala	Panama	Panama
2nd Choice	Costa Rica	Costa Rica	Bahamas	Florida Keys	Bahamas	Cancun, Mexico	Florida Keys	Venezuela	Mazatlan	Panama	Costa Rica	Costa Rica
Other			Costa Rica						Panama			

Author Biographies

Brion Babbitt of Dennisville, New Jersey, is a charter boat captain and free-lance outdoor writer and photographer with credits in dozens of magazines. He has fished from Massachusetts to Florida and Mexico, and written for *Salt Water Sportsman* magazine since 1987. His charter boat, *Makoman*, is in Cape May, New Jersey.

Scott Boyan is a former Associate Editor of *Salt Water Sportsman* magazine. During his tenure, he edited and wrote for several departments, as well as many feature articles. Boyan now resides in Isla Mujeres, Mexico, with his wife Maria. When he isn't running his hotel, Secreto, Boyan enjoys pursuing sailfish and tarpon.

John Brownlee is a native Floridian who grew up fishing the waters of the Gulf of Mexico north of Tampa for king and Spanish mackerel, speckled trout and redfish. He has since expanded his angling horizons to include fishing excursions throughout the coastal United States, Mexico, Central America, the Caribbean and the Bahamas. A dedicated conservationist, Brownlee and his family moved to Islamorada, Florida, to indulge themselves in the incredible fishing opportunities available in the Florida Keys. He currently serves as the Upper Keys IGFA representative, the sportfishing representative on the Florida Keys National Marine Sanctuary Advisory Council and as a Senior Editor for *Salt Water Sportsman* magazine.

John Cacciutti can be found fishing from his boat *Marathon John* along the East Coast of the United States. He is a frequent contributor to *Salt Water Sportsman* magazine and has spent numerous hours on the water refining his techniques for catching billfish.

Mitch Chagnon, a native of Rhode Island, has plied the waters of New England for over 40 years. He is a well-respected charter captain who possesses an intimate knowledge of both offshore and inshore grounds, and works closely with various conservation and sportfishing groups. In addition to his chartering work, Chagnon lectures at many sporting shows.

Angelo Cuanang is the 45-year-old San Francisco Bay Regional Editor for *Salt Water Sportsman* magazine and has fished for, photographed and written articles on a large variety of popular salt water gamefish. His photos and features have appeared in all the major West Coast fishing publications. Although he enjoys fishing other great locations like Baja, Alaska and Costa Rica, Angelo does most of his fishing in the San Francisco Bay area for stripers, salmon, halibut and sturgeon. He does most of his fishing from a Boston Whaler.

Chuck Garrison has been a sportfishing photojournalist for more than 30 years. During his career he has held field editorships with *Field & Stream, Outdoor Life, Salt Water Sportsman* and *South Coast Sportfishing* magazines. He has written more than a thousand feature articles and authored five salt water fishing books, including his best-selling, *Offshore Fishing Southern California and Baja.*

Barry Gibson is the long-time Editor of *Salt Water Sportsman* magazine. He has been a charter boat captain in Boothbay Harbor, Maine, since 1971, and currently guides exclusively for striped bass and bluefish from his 24-foot center-console. He has served as a government fishery manager, has fished extensively in North and South America, and contributes to a variety of outdoor publications.

Jim Hendricks, a native of southern California, has fished the local waters his entire life. His specialty is inshore fishing. He is a frequent contributor to numerous sportfishing publications including *Salt Water Sportsman* and *South Coast Sportfishing* and is Editor of *Trailer Boats* magazine.

Capt. Michael "Beak" Hurt has long been recognized as one of the top blue water fishermen on the California/Mexico big game circuit. The "Beak", as he is known throughout the industry, has fished all his life and has been a licensed skipper for nearly three decades. Beak's credentials, successes on the water and his very impressive tournament portfolio are why his consultation seminars and

"how to" articles are in big demand. As West Coast Editor for *Marlin Magazine* in the mid-80s, he was more of an ambassador than a writer. Soon, his articles became recognized for helping all captains and anglers to better understand the commonalties of our fisheries. Moving to *Sportfishing Magazine*, he expanded on this position and joined *Salt Water Sportsman* as their Offshore Editor. His concern for the industry is further exemplified by his efforts in working with the conservation organizations that fight for the betterment of our fisheries. He is now the Southern California Representative for the RFA.

Mike Moore is an accomplished photojournalist whose work appears in the world's most respected angling publications. Mike specializes in stand-up, big-game fishing with deep roots as a licensed captain. Mike is also a professional fireman who enjoys fishing on their 25-foot Skipjack, *Legacy*, off California with wife Lindy and daughters Kelsey and Delaney.

John E. Phillips has written and sold 22 books on the outdoors, more than 10,000 newspaper columns, 5,000 magazine articles and 20,000 photos. He has had a radio show airing on 28 stations and has taught seminars in colleges, at writer's meetings and for the Outdoor Writers Association of America. John is also the outdoor writer for the *Birmingham Post-Herald* newspaper, and his work appears monthly in national and regional publications. Additionally, he does daily uploads for five outdoor companies websites.

George Poveromo is a renowned angling authority who serves as a Senior Editor for *Salt Water Sportsman* magazine. In addition to producing and hosting the *Salt Water Sportsman* National Seminar Series — the nation's largest and most successful educational course on marine fishing techniques — he is also the Executive Producer and Host of *George Poveromo's World of Saltwater Fishing*, which airs on ESPN2.

Tom Richardson is Managing Editor of *Salt Water Sportsman* magazine. In addition to his photo and article contributions to *SWS*, Richardson is a freelance writer and photographer, as well as a contributing writer to the on-line fishing magazine *Reel-time*. Tom pursues a number of salt water fish species and spends most of his time on the waters of southern Massachusetts, Cape Cod and Rhode Island.

Allan J. (Al) Ristori started salt water fishing 55 years ago and began writing about it for national and regional magazines in 1965. He has written thousands of articles and is in his 17th year as Salt Water Editor of the *Newark Star-Ledger*. His books include *North American Saltwater Fishing, The Saltwater Fish Identifier* and *Fishing for Bluefish*, in addition to sections in *Striped Bass Fishing: Salt Water Strategies* and *Inshore Salt Water Fishing*. Ristori is a charter captain who fishes out of Point Pleasant, New Jersey for everything from stripers and blues to tuna and sharks. He currently serves as *Salt Water Sportsman's* New York/New Jersey Editor.

Jim Rizzuto has written thousands of newspaper and magazine articles and eight books about fishing in Hawaii. He is the author and publisher of *The Kona Fishing Chronicles* series, *Modern Hawaiian Gamefishing* and the three-volume *Fishing Hawaii Style* series. His weekly column appears in the Kona newspaper *West Hawaii Today*, and his monthly column in *Hawaii Fishing News*. Since he began writing for magazines 35 years ago, his articles have appeared in numerous outdoor publications.

Tom Waters is Southwest Regional Editor for *Salt Water Sportsman* magazine. Tom is an accomplished writer, artist/illustrator, photographer and lecturer who specializes in sportfishing and has fished Pacific waters from Alaska to Mexico and Hawaii. He was a fishing lure manufacturer for nearly a decade and has served as an Editor to four different sportfishing magazines. Tom and his wife Sherry enjoy travel, fishing and photography and also operate their own graphic design studio.

Photo & Illustration Credits

PHOTOGRAPHERS

(Note: T=Top, C=Center, B=Bottom, L=Left, R=Right)

Dan Blanton
DanBlanton.com
© Dan Blanton: p. 97

William Boyce
Boyceimage.com
© William Boyce: back cover L, pp. 68, 80, 96

Richard Gibson
Homestead, FL
© Richard Gibson/High Seas Photography:
pp. 3B, 47, 82-83, 119

Richard Herrmann
Poway, CA
© Randy Morse/Herrmann Pix: p. 111
© Richard Herrmann: p. 112

Scott Kerrigan
ScottKerrigan.com
© Scott Kerrigan: back cover R, pp. 3BC, 8, 54, 87, 94

Gary Kramer
Willows, CA
© Gary Kramer: p. 18

Larry Larsen
Lakeland, FL
© Larry Larsen: p. 115

Evelyn Letfuss
New York, NY
© Evelyn Letfuss: cover BL, pp. 3T, 6, 21, 36, 53, 84

Bill Lindner Photography
St. Paul, MN
© Bill Lindner Photography: back cover C, pp. 4, 12, 25, 27, 33, 56, 90

Dick Mermon
Spring Hill, FL
© Dick Mermon: p. 92

Tony Peña
Spring Valley, CA
© Tony Peña: pp. 60, 100

George Poveromo
Parkland, FL
© George Poveromo: pp. 28, 29, 89B, 103, 106

Tom Richardson
Brookline, MA
© Tom Richardson: cover BR, p. 72

Al Ristori
Manasquan Park, NJ
© Al Ristori: pp. 50, 75, 78

Philip Rosenberg
Holualoa, HI
© Philip Rosenberg: p. 14

Lenny Rudow
Edgewater, MD
© Rudow Photo: p. 89T

David J. Sams
DavidJSams.com
© David J. Sams/Texas Inprint: pp. 24, 26, 63, 66

Seapics.com
Kailua-Kona, HI
© Mark Conlin: cover background photo
© Eleonora de Sabata: p. 30
© Richard Herrmann: pp. 3TC, 34

Bob Stearns
Boca Raton, FL
© Bob Stearns/Ocean Arts, Inc.: p. 40

Sam Talarico
Mohnton, PA
© Sam Talarico: p. 41

Art Womack
awfoto.com
© Art Womack: p. 43

ILLUSTRATORS

Chris Armstrong
Jacksonville, FL
© Chris Armstrong: pp. 38-39, 71

Dan Daly
Camden, ME
© Dan Daly: p. 62

John F. Eggert
Chicago, IL
© John F. Eggert: pp. 91-93

Joe Fahey
Minneapolis, MN
© Joe Fahey: pp. 8, 15, 80

Dave McHose
West Palm Beach, FL
© Dave McHose: pp. 32, 59, 101

Diane Rome Peebles*
St. Petersburg, FL
© Diane Rome Peebles: pp. 7, 35, 55, 122-125

Don Ray
DonRayStudio.com
© Don Ray: cover painting

John Rice
New York, NY
© John Rice: pp. 65, 98

David Shepherd
Narragansett, RI
© David Shepherd: pp. 41, 46, 104, 105

Tom Waters
Carlsbad, CA
© Tom Waters: pp. 44, 45, 77, 81, 86, 114

* Some of Diane Rome Peebles illustrations appear courtesy of the Florida Fish & Wildlife Conservation Commission.

Creative Publishing international is the most complete source of How-To Information for the Outdoorsman

THE COMPLETE HUNTER™ *Series*

- *Advanced Whitetail Hunting*
- *America's Favorite Wild Game Recipes*
- *Bowhunting Equipment & Skills*
- *The Complete Guide to Hunting*
- *Cooking Wild in Kate's Kitchen*
- *Dressing & Cooking Wild Game*
- *Duck Hunting*
- *Elk Hunting*
- *Game Bird Cookery*
- *Mule Deer Hunting*
- *Muzzleloading*
- *Pronghorn Hunting*
- *Venison Cookery*
- *Whitetail Deer*
- *Whitetail Techniques & Tactics*
- *Wild Turkey*

The Freshwater Angler™ *Series*

- *Advanced Bass Fishing*
- *All-Time Favorite Fish Recipes*
- *The Art of Fly Tying*
- *The Art of Freshwater Fishing*
- *Fishing for Catfish*
- *Fishing Rivers & Streams*
- *Fishing Tips & Tricks*
- *Fishing With Artificial Lures*
- *Fishing With Live Bait*
- *Fly Fishing for Trout in Streams*
- *Largemouth Bass*
- *Modern Methods of Ice Fishing*
- *The New Cleaning & Cooking Fish*
- *Northern Pike & Muskie*
- *Panfish*
- *Smallmouth Bass*
- *Successful Walleye Fishing*
- *Trout*

The Complete FLY FISHERMAN™ *Series*

- *Fishing Dry Flies – Surface Presentations for Trout in Streams*
- *Fishing Nymphs, Wet Flies & Streamers – Subsurface Techniques for Trout in Streams*
- *Fly-Fishing Equipment & Skills*
- *Fly-Tying Techniques & Patterns*

To purchase these or other titles,
contact your local bookseller, call **1-800-328-3895**
or visit our web site at **www.creativepub.com**

For a list of participating retailers near you, call 1-800-328-0590